Basic Accounting

Steve Dix

RAVAN PRESS

Published in 1997 by Ravan Press
PO Box 32484 Braamfontein 2017 South Africa

Reprinted 2000

© Steve Dix

Cover design: Centre Court Studio
Typesetting: Pat de Zeeuw cc

ISBN 0 86975 504 8

Printed by Creda Communications,
Eliot Avenue, Eppindust II, Cape Town
66598

Contents

This course is an introduction to Practical Accounting. It is written in a simple style and requires that you participate in the process of learning throughout the course. You will learn how to write up accounting records for a small business. Enjoy it!

Please take note of this:
The terminology that is used in this book is the same as that used in the business environment. However, you may find that other books or accounting courses make use of different words to describe the same things. In this regard, please note the following alternative ways of describing some of the books of first entry (subsidiary books):

Terminology used in this book:	Alternative terminology:
The Cash Receipts section of the Cash Book	The Cash Receipts Journal
The Cash Payments section of the Cash Book	The Cash Payments Journal
The Sales Journal	The Debtors' Journal
The Sales Returns Journal	The Debtors' Allowances Journal
The Purchases Journal	The Creditors' Journal
The Purchases Returns Journal	The Creditors' Allowances Journal

CHAPTER ONE

Introduction to Accounting

A. INTRODUCTION

Working with money is a part of everyone's life. We earn money and we spend it. Every person and household should keep a record of how much is earned and how those earnings are spent. Do you keep a record of your money?

A business also earns and spends money. However, a business must keep a complete record of its finances. At all times, the business manager must know how profitable the business is. He or she must know how much money there is in the bank and how much money the business owes or is owed. Keeping the financial records of the business is the responsibility of the Accounting Department.

The objective of this course is to give you an understanding of accounting and to provide you with the skills necessary to record the accounting transactions for a small business.

B. ACCOUNTING DEFINED

Accounting is the process of keeping a record of all business transactions. A transaction is a business deal, for example, the sale of goods or a payment to a supplier.

In a cricket match, the job of the scorekeeper is to keep track of how well each team is doing. In business, the accountant is the scorekeeper. The accountant's job is to keep "score" of all business transactions.

C. THE ACCOUNTING PERIOD

Time is an important part of record keeping. For example, a business manager may be interested in how much was sold in the month of January 1997. Or how much was paid in wages for the six months ended 30 June 1996. Or how much profit was made in the year ended 31 December 1996.

The time period must always be stated. It makes no sense to say we sold R1 000 worth of goods unless we state the period of time over which this occurred. This period of time is called the accounting period.

A business operates over a cycle or period of twelve months. This period is called the financial year. The financial year may run from 1 January to 31 December. More commonly, it can run from 1 March to 28 February of the following calendar year. The last day of the financial year is called the **financial year end**.

D. ACCOUNTING IS A "DOING" SUBJECT

Accounting is a subject that demands a lot of practice and "doing". No one has ever mastered accounting by reading a book or by listening to a tape. You will only master this subject by doing the exercises at the end of each chapter.

Each chapter builds on the chapter(s) before it. So make sure that you understand each chapter completely before you move on to the next one.

1

CHAPTER TWO

Basic Accounting Concepts and Terminology

A. INTRODUCTION

Starting to learn accounting is like learning a new language. You must first learn some new words. You should read through this chapter at least three times and make sure that you understand the meaning of each term.

Let's suppose that you are the owner of a small furniture store. You buy furniture from a manufacturer. You mark-up the price so that you make a profit when you sell the furniture to the consumer. THE COMMODITIES THAT YOU BUY TO RESELL ARE CALLED YOUR GOODS, MERCHANDISE OR TRADING STOCK. Since you are in the business of selling furniture, the furniture is called your "goods" or "trading stock".

We will now discuss four very important terms that you must know: Assets, Liabilities, Expenses and Income.

B. ASSETS

Assets are those things that belong to your business, i.e. they are the possessions of the business. For example, you may own the shop and the land on which it is built. You may have a delivery vehicle, some cash in the bank and a stock of goods (furniture). These are all examples of assets.

There are two different types of assets. They are called **fixed assets** and **current assets**.

1. Current assets

Current assets are either in cash form or they will soon be converted into cash (money) within the forthcoming financial year. Examples of current assets are money in the bank and cash in the petty cash box. These are examples of current assets that are already in cash form.

Other examples of current assets are "stock of unsold goods" and "debtors". These are current assets that will be converted into cash within the next financial year. Once stock of goods is sold for cash, the asset **stock** is converted into cash. A **debtor** is a customer who owes you money. When the debtor pays his debt, you receive cash.

2. Fixed assets

Fixed assets are not easily converted to cash. These are assets which the business will keep and use for more than one year. For example, ownership of land and buildings is a fixed asset. Any vehicles that the business owns are also fixed assets.

In accounting, we put certain fixed assets into groups or categories. For example, photocopy machines, typewriters, calculators and computers are called **office equipment**. Chairs, tables and desks that are used in the business are called *office furniture*.

Remember that our example was that of a furniture shop. The furniture that is used in the business by the staff members is a fixed asset. However, the furniture that is on display to be sold or that is in the warehouse is called **trading stock** or **goods**. This is a current asset.

C. LIABILITIES

A liability is the opposite of an asset. Whereas an asset is something that your business owns, a liability is money that your business owes to somebody else.

We can distinguish between current liabilities and long-term liabilities.

Current liabilities
A current liability is a debt that must be repaid within one year. An example of a current liability is a creditor. This is a person (or another business) to whom your store owes money, and who will be repaid within the next year.

Long-term liabilities
Long-term liabilities are debts that are repayable over a period longer than one year. An example of a long-term liability is a loan from a bank that is to be repaid over a period of many years.

Capital
When you first started your furniture store, you invested some money in the business to get it going. Any money or anything else of value that you, the owner, invest in your business is called CAPITAL.

As owner of the business, you can close the business and take out your investment (as well as any profits that the business has made for you). Since you have a claim over the capital that you invested, we can think of capital as a long-term liability that the business has to its owner.

D. EXPENSES

Expenses are those costs necessary to run the business efficiently. Expenses usually arise on an ongoing basis, such as monthly or yearly. What expenses would the owner of a furniture store incur? Write these down in the think box below.

Some of the more common expenses in any business are shop rental, telephone, electricity and water, advertising, insurance, salaries, wages and cleaning materials. However, there are other expenses that are not as obvious. Let's look at some of these:

Depreciation
Fixed assets (other than property) are worth less and less as time goes by. For example, you pay R4 000 for a photocopy machine today. As time goes by, the machine becomes outdated and old and its value drops. We say that the asset has depreciated. Each financial year, the amount by which the asset has depreciated is shown as an expense. If we depreciate the photocopier by 25% each year, then we will "write off" R1 000 depreciation per year. This means that the asset is worth R1 000 less each year. Depreciation is an expense that does not involve the actual payment of money from the business.

Drawings
The owner of the business can take money or value out of the business. This withdrawal from the business by the owner is called **drawings**. This is an expense to the business.

Motor vehicle running expenses
The motor vehicle that is owned by the business is a fixed asset. However, the car needs a licence, petrol and may need repairs. These are all expenses that are necessary to keep the car running.

Purchases
This is an expense that is incurred only when we **buy goods** to resell at a profit. In the case of a furniture shop, purchases means that we have bought furniture in order to resell it. For a clothing business, purchases means that clothes have been bought for resale. The goods that are left over at the end of the month or year are called **stock**.

E. INCOME

Income (or revenue) is the opposite of expenses. While expenses are generally money flowing out of the business, income is money coming into the business. What types of income might a business receive?

Sales
The most important form of income is sales. This is the income that comes from the **sale of goods**. When our furniture shop sells its goods, this is called sales.

Rent received
Assume that you are not using all the space in your furniture shop. There is an area at the back of the shop that is of no use to you. Now, if the owner of a nearby shop offers you R300 per month rental to make use of this space, what would you do? Of course, you will rent it out! Each month, you will receive R300 rental income. This income is called **rent received**.

Other sources of income include **discount received** when we pay our suppliers on time. **Interest received** is that income from earning interest on our investments.

4

F.   THE PROFITS OF A BUSINESS

The reason that you started your furniture store was to make a PROFIT. Your profit comes from buying the furniture at one price and selling it at a higher price.

The profit that the business makes belongs to you, the owner. As a business makes profit, the owner's stake in the business increases. (The business will "owe" the owner more).

Calculating the gross profit

But how are the profits of a business calculated? To deal with this question, let's use an example:

> Assume that you are the owner of a bicycle retailer. Since you are in the business of selling bicycles, they are called your TRADING STOCK or GOODS. You make a profit by buying the bicycles (purchases) from a wholesaler and then selling them (sales) at a higher price to the consumer. This is called your GROSS PROFIT (or gross margin).

Example 2.1

If you buy 10 bikes at R50 each and sell the 10 bikes for R80 each, how much gross profit have you made?

Purchases: 10 bikes × R50 = R500
Sales: 10 bikes × R80 = R800
Gross Profit = Sales − Purchases
Gross Profit = R800 − R500
Gross Profit = R300

Exercise 2.1

Calculate your total profit if you buy 5 bikes at R50 each and sell them at R70 each?

Calculation Box

Another way of looking at the above calculation is to multiply the number of bikes sold by the profit made on each bike. You make a profit of R20 on each bike sold since you buy at R50 and sell at R70. If you sell 5 bikes at a profit of R20 per bike, that means that your total profit is R100 (5 × R20).

5

Calculating the net profit

After making a gross profit on the sale of the bikes, the owner must still pay for the expenses of the business. The rental on the shop, insurance, electricity and salaries must now be deducted from the gross profit. In addition, any income (other than sales), must be added on to the gross profit. The amount left over is called the NET PROFIT of the business.

During 1996, a business makes a gross profit of R50 000. The expenses of the business are rent (R15 000), salaries (R12 000), electricity and water (R1 200) and advertising (R800). Discount received amounts to R500. Calculate the net profit for 1996.

Calculation Box

G. OWNER'S EQUITY

As the owner of a business, you will want to know how much your investment in the business is worth at any one time. This is called **owner's equity.** It can be calculated by three components:

1. Capital

Remember that capital is the initial amount that the owner invests into the business. The owner can also invest additional capital into the business as necessary.

2. Net profit

Why do people open businesses? They believe that the business will make a net profit. This profit belongs to the business owner(s) who took the risk of starting the business. Therefore net profit increases the amount owing to the owner. If the business makes a net loss, then the owner's equity decreases.

3. Drawings

This is the opposite of a capital investment. Drawings occur when the owner **takes out** money or value from the business. Drawings reduce the owner's investment in the business.

Owners Equity = Capital + Net Profit − Drawings

It is extremely important that you have a thorough understanding of the contents of this chapter. What is discussed here will be the foundation for the rest of the book.

6

Study this chapter a number of times until you have fully grasped the terminology and concepts.

Test-yourself questions

Question 2.1

In the table supplied, fill in examples under each category heading. Write in as many examples of fixed assets, current assets, long-term liabilities, current liabilities, expenses and income that you can think of.

ASSETS	LIABILITIES	EXPENSES	INCOME
Fixed	Long-term		
Current	Current		

Question 2.2

The following accounting items have come to your attention:

Capital, Petty Cash, Sales, Creditors, Land and Buildings, Bank, Commission Received, Purchases, Vehicles, Loan from ABC Bank, Rates and Taxes, Machinery and Equipment, Bank Charges, Debtors.

Write each of the above names alongside the category to which they belong on the table supplied:

CATEGORY	NAME OF ACCOUNT
Fixed assets Current assets Long-term liabilities Current liabilities Expenses Income	

Question 2.3

Delete the incorrect option or fill in the missing word for the following:

(a)   Expenses increase/decrease the profits of the business.
(b)   Sales increase/decrease the profits of the business.
(c)   Customers who owe money to a business are called creditors/debtors.

(d)   Money taken from the business by the owner for his or her personal use is called:

_____.

(e)   Fixed assets are long-term/short-term possessions.

(f)   Capital is the investment by the owner in the business. It can also be thought of as the long-term liability that the business has to its owner. True or false?

(g)   When a business buys goods for resale, we call this purchases/trading stock.

(h)   The goods left over at the end of a financial period (month or year) are called purchases/stock.

CHAPTER THREE

The Double Entry System

A. INTRODUCTION

From Chapter 2, you should know some basic accounting terms. Now, we begin with the basics of accounting. In this chapter, we look at how business events or transactions are entered into an account.

B. WHAT IS AN ACCOUNT?

All businesses have a book called the ledger. The ledger keeps a record or an account of each asset, liability, expense and income in the business. For example, there is an account for vehicles. This account tells you the value of vehicles the business owns. The Capital account tells you how much the business "owes" to the owner. The Stationery account tells you how much has been spent on stationery.

The set-out of an account
Each account is in the shape of a **T**. The left hand side is called the **debit side**, and the right hand side is called the **credit side**.

Debit side   Credit side

When you write something on the left hand side of the account, this is known as debiting the account. We say that a debit entry is put through or that the account is **debited**.

When you write something on the right hand side of the account, this is known as crediting the account. We say that a credit entry is put through or that the account is **credited**.

The name of the account is written on top of the account in the middle. So the Vehicles account would look as follows:

Debit side   VEHICLES ACCOUNT   Credit side

C. THE EFFECTS OF DEBITING OR CREDITING AN ACCOUNT

We have already said that each account has two sides — a debit side on the left, and a credit side on the right.

We have also said that when you write something on the debit side (left hand side), you are debiting the account.

When you write something on the credit side (right hand side), you are crediting the account.

But what does it mean to debit or credit an account? This depends on whether the account is an asset, a liability, expenses or income.

1. Asset accounts

The rule for all asset accounts is simple:

> If you want to show that an asset account has *increased*, you must put through **a debit entry**. This means that you write something on the left hand side.

For example, on Jan 3, the amount of money in your bank account is increased by R100. This must be entered on the debit side of the bank account (since bank is an asset account and assets are increased by debit entries).

Debit side	BANK ACCOUNT	Credit side
1997 Jan 3 100,00		

This rule applies to all asset accounts. To show an increase in Land and Buildings, Furniture, Vehicles, Equipment, Debtors, Petty Cash or any other asset, the asset account must be debited.

Since the debit and credit side are opposites, the reverse is also true:

> If you want to show that an asset account has *decreased*, you must put through **a credit entry**. This means that you will write something on the right hand side.

2. Liability accounts

Since a liability is the opposite of an asset, the rule for liabilities is the opposite of the asset rule:

> If you want to show that a liability account has *increased*, you must put through **a credit entry**. This means that you will write something on the right hand side.

For example, if on Jan 15, you take a R10 000 loan from **The Development Corporation**, you will have increased your liabilities or debts. The loan account must now be credited in order to show that liabilities have increased.

Debit side	LOAN FROM DEVELOPMENT CORPORATION	Credit side
	1997 Jan 15	10 000,00

Once again the reverse is also true:

> If you want to show that a liability account has *decreased*, you must put through **a debit entry**. This means that you will write something on the left hand side.

Since capital is really a **liability to the owner**, it makes sense that the capital account is also increased by means of a credit entry and reduced by means of a debit entry.

3. Expenses

The rule for expenses is as follows:

> If you want to show that an expense account has *increased*, you must put through a **debit** entry. This means that you write something on the left hand side.

For example, if on Jan 21, you incur an expense of R500 for salaries, then this must be entered on the debit side of the salaries account.

Debit side	SALARIES	Credit side
1997 Jan 21 500,00		

Since the debit and credit side are opposites, the reverse is also true:

> If you want to show that an expense has *decreased*, you must put through a credit entry to the expense account. This means that you will write something on the right hand side.

4. Income

The rule for income is as follows:

> If you want to show that an income account has *increased*, you must put through a **credit entry**. This means that you write something on the right hand side.

For example, if on Jan 27, you earn income of R1 000 for sales, then this must be entered on the credit side of the sales account.

Debit side	SALES	Credit side
	1997 Jan 27	1 000,00

Since the debit and credit side are opposites, the reverse is also true:

> If you want to show that income has *decreased*, you must put through a debit entry to the income account. This means that you will write something on the left hand side.

These rules are very important and you must make sure that you know them fully before continuing. The rules can be summarised as follows:

ASSETS ARE INCREASED BY DEBIT ENTRIES.

EXPENSES ARE INCREASED BY DEBIT ENTRIES.

LIABILITIES ARE INCREASED BY CREDIT ENTRIES.

INCOME ACCOUNTS ARE INCREASED BY CREDIT ENTRIES.

You can easily remember this by using the word **AEDLIC**.

AEDLIC:
Assets and Expenses are Debits when they increase, Liabilities and Income are Credits when they increase.

Exercise 3.1
For each of the following accounts, indicate whether the account increases by means of a debit or a credit entry:

Tick either the debit or the credit column:

Name of account	Debit	Credit
Stationery		
Capital		
Petty cash		
Loan — XYZ Bank		
Joe Bloggs (debtor)		
Electricity and water		
Rent received		
Purchases		
Drawings		
Rent		
Rick Quale (creditor)		
Sales		
Land and buildings		

Take special note that you can never have a ledger account called **asset, liability, expenses or income.** The account must be named as specifically as possible. For example, you can have a ledger account called **bank** or one called **petty cash**. From these labels, you know that the account is a current asset. (But you never name the account "current asset".)

CHAPTER FOUR

An Exercise in Double Entry

A. INTRODUCTION

This chapter gives an example of how a set of accounts is written up. You will see how the double entry system works. This is a very important chapter. Study it again and again until you fully understand the principle of double entry.

B. BUSINESS TRANSACTIONS

A transaction is an action between two parties. For example, if you buy goods from a supplier, two parties are involved — you and the supplier. If you sell goods to a customer, two parties are involved — you and the customer.

   When you record the transactions of the business, always think of yourself as the owner of that business.

C. THE DOUBLE ENTRY SYSTEM

There is a unique way in which accounting transactions are recorded. It is called the double entry system.

   It means that for one business transaction, an entry is made in two accounts. One account is debited while the other account is credited.

   Therefore, when an account is debited, another account must be credited at the same time. This means that the total debits are always equal to the total credits in the ledger.

D. BOB'S BICYCLE SHOP — AN EXERCISE IN DOUBLE ENTRY

Bobby Bluebell opens a business called "Bob's Bicycle Shop". The purpose of the business is to buy and sell bicycles. Remember that you must put yourself in the position of the owner of the business. Imagine that you are Bobby Bluebell.

Transaction 1
On 3 January 1997, Bobby goes to the bank, opens up an account in the name of "Bob's Bicycle Shop", and deposits an amount of R1 000 as capital. This is the first transaction for the new business. The transaction is between Bobby and his bank.

January 3: The owner deposits capital of R1 000 into the bank
This one transaction affects two accounts (double entry).
1. Firstly, the money in the business bank account is increased. The asset **bank** is increased. Since an increase in an asset is shown by means of a debit entry, the **bank account** must be **debited**.
2. Secondly, the owner's capital is increased. Since this is a liability (debt) by the business to the owner, the **capital** account must be **credited**.

The debit entry in the bank account is written as follows:

Debit side				BANK ACCOUNT	Credit side
1997					
Jan 3	Capital		1 000,00		
A	B	C	D		

A. The "date" column
This is the date on which the transaction took place. Note that the year is written above the month, and both are in the same column. The day is written alongside the month.

B. The "details" column
In this transaction, the two accounts involved are bank and capital. In the details column of the bank account, you will write the name of the other account "capital". This tells you why money was deposited into the bank.

C. The "folio" column
This column gives the source of the transaction. For now, you can ignore this column.

D. The "amount" column.
The value of the transaction is written here in rands and cents.

The entry in the bank account is now a meaningful accounting statement. It tells you that **bank** (name of account) was increased (debit side) by R1 000 on 1 Jan 1997 by means of a capital contribution (details).

The other part of the entry is a credit to the capital account.

Debit side	CAPITAL ACCOUNT		Credit side
	1997		
	Jan 3	Bank	1 000,00

The details of the transaction are written on the credit side of the capital account. Note that the name of the other account **bank** is written in the "details" column of the capital account.

The entry in the capital account reads as follows: "The Capital account (name of the account) has increased (credited) by R1 000 on 3 Jan 1997 by means of a deposit in the bank (details)."

Transaction 2
Bobby now finds a small shop to rent. The shop is on the street front and Bobby hopes to attract passing trade. He now needs some furniture for the shop. So he enters into another transaction:

January 4: Bob's Bicycle Shop buys a desk and a chair for R200
In accounting, similar items are always grouped into a single category. Desks, chairs, tables and other similar objects all fall into the category of **furniture**.

Can you think of the double effect of this transaction?

Firstly, there is an increase in the amount of furniture that the business owns. The asset **furniture** is increased. The **furniture** account must be **debited**.

Debit side		OFFICE FURNITURE ACCOUNT			Credit side
1997					
Jan 4	Bank	200,00			

Secondly, there is a decrease in the amount of money in the bank. The asset **bank** is decreased. Therefore, the **bank** account must be **credited**.

Debit side		BANK ACCOUNT			Credit side
1997			1997		
Jan 3	Capital	1 000,00	Jan 4	Office furniture	200,00

Notice that we do not open another bank account. All bank entries are entered into the same bank account. Go back and look at the bank account. Do you see that there is R800 left in the bank (R1 000 less R200)? This is known as **the balance on the bank account** or simply **the bank balance**.

Transaction 3

Now, Bobby needs to buy a cash register (a till). He is informed that they cost R100. He does not want to pay out any more cash since he still has to buy stocks of bicycles. So he phones up Office Supplies (Pty) Ltd and places an order to buy a cash register on credit (on account). This means that he takes possession of the cash register now, but will only pay for it at some future date. Until such time that he pays for it, Office Supplies (Pty) Ltd is Bob's creditor.

January 5: Bought a cash register on credit from Office Supplies (Pty) Ltd for R100

Assets such as photocopiers, typewriters, calculators and cash registers all fall into the category of **office equipment**.

This transaction has the effect of increasing the office equipment. The asset **office equipment** is increased. Therefore the **office equipment account** must be **debited**.

The entry on the debit side of the office equipment account is as follows:

Debit side		OFFICE EQUIPMENT			Credit side
1997					
Jan 5	Office Supplies	100,00			

The business now owes money to a creditor called **Office Supplies (Pty) Ltd**. Since creditors are liabilities, we must put through a credit entry to show that liabilities have increased. But, in order to show that the money is owed to **Office Supplies (Pty) Ltd**, we must credit their account.

The entry on the credit side of the **Office Supplies** account is as follows:

Debit side	OFFICE SUPPLIES (PTY) LTD		Credit side
	1997		
	Jan 5	Office Equipment	100,00

This can be identified as a creditor's account since the account is in the name of a person or a business and it has a credit balance.

Transaction 4

Until now, Bob has been concerned with setting up his business, and laying out his shop. But now it is time to start trading in bicycles. The business must start to pay for itself by making a profit.

Bob phones up a supplier of bicycles called Bikes Unlimited and he orders 10 bicycles at R50 each. The salesperson at Bikes Unlimited informs Bob that he must pay cash for these bicycles.

January 6: Bought 10 bicycles for R500 from Bikes Unlimited and paid by cheque

By buying the bicycles, Bob has increased his purchases. Remember that we described purchases as the **buying of goods**. Remember, too, that purchases is an expense to the business. Since expenses are debits, the **purchases** account must be **debited**.

The other part to this transaction is that Bob's money in the bank is reduced. The **bank** account must be credited.

Try putting this double entry through yourself.

Debit side	PURCHASES ACCOUNT	Credit side

Debit side	BANK ACCOUNT		Credit side
1997		1997	
Jan 3 Capital 1 000,00		Jan 4 Office furniture 200,00	

It is not necessary to repeat the year or month in the bank account since they have not changed.

Transaction 5

Bob is now ready to sell. His shop is furnished, he has a cash register and 10 bicycles for sale. He now waits for customers.

Bob's first customer arrives and, after some discussion, agrees to buy one bicycle for R80.

January 10: Sold a bicycle for cash (R80)

Bob's money increases by R80 which is deposited into the bank account the next morning. The **bank** account must be **debited**.

Bob's sales have increased by R80. Sales is an income account and therefore it must be **credited**.

16

Put these entries through yourself:

Debit side			BANK ACCOUNT		Credit side
1997			1997		
Jan 3	Capital	1 000,00	Jan 4	Office furniture	200,00
			6	Purchases	500,00

Debit side	SALES ACCOUNT	Credit side

Transaction 6

A few days later, John Crossbar comes into the shop to inspect the bicycles. He tells Bob that he is the president of a cycling club that needs 6 bicycles for new members. John has no problem with the price of R80 per bike, but is unable to pay cash upfront. John will pay for the bikes at the end of the month. Bob agrees to sell the bikes on credit to John Crossbar.

January 11: Sold 6 bicycles on credit to John Crossbar for R480

John Crossbar has bought the goods and will settle up at the end of the month. He is Bob's debtor. Remember that debtors are assets. To show the increase in debtors, **John Crossbar's account** must be **debited**. Note that we debit the name of the person who owes the money.

Since sales are increased, the **sales** account must be **credited**. It does not matter whether the goods are sold for cash or on credit. The same sales account must be credited.

Put these entries through below:

Debit side	JOHN CROSSBAR ACCOUNT	Credit side

Debit side		SALES ACCOUNT		Credit side
		1997		
		Jan 10	Bank	80,00

Transaction 7

Over the next few days, no more bicycles are sold. So Bob decides to advertise his business in a local newspaper. The cost of the advertisement is R50. He settles up immediately, paying by cheque.

January 13: Paid R50 to *The Chronicle* Newspaper for an advertisement

Advertising is an expense. It is a cost of running the business. Since expenses are debits, the **advertising** account must be **debited**.

The bank balance is also decreased since R50 is paid out. The **bank** account must be **credited**.

Put through these entries:

Debit side	ADVERTISING ACCOUNT		Credit side

Debit side			BANK ACCOUNT		Credit side
1997			1997		
Jan 3	Capital	1 000,00	Jan 4	Office furniture	200,00
10	Sales	80,00	6	Purchases	500,00

Transaction 8

Bob is asked to sub-let the back room of his shop to the next-door shopkeeper. He agrees to do this since he is not making any use of the back room at present. They agree upon a rental of R30 for the rest of January. This amount is payable immediately.

January 17: Received an amount of R30 as rental for an unused back room

The incoming R30 increases Bob's bank balance (assets increase). The bank account must be _____.

Rent received is income to Bob's Bikes. Since income accounts are credits, the **rent received** account must be **credited**.

Put through these entries:

Debit side	RENT RECEIVED ACCOUNT		Credit side

Debit side			BANK ACCOUNT		Credit side
1997			1997		
Jan 3	Capital	1 000,00	Jan 4	Office furniture	200,00
10	Sales	80,00	6	Purchases	500,00
			13	Advertising	50,00

Transactions 9 and 10

At the end of the first month of trading, Bob pays out two amounts of money. Shop rental for January amounts to R80. Electricity and Water for the month amounts to R30.

18

January 27: Paid R80 for shop rental
January 30: Paid R30 for electricity and water

Rent and electricity are both expenses. Therefore, both accounts must be debited. Since money is being spent, the bank account must be credited for both payments.

Put through these entries:

Debit side		RENT ACCOUNT		Credit side	

Debit side		ELECTRICITY AND WATER		Credit side	

Debit side		BANK ACCOUNT			Credit side	
1997			1997			
Jan 3	Capital	1 000,00	Jan 4	Office furniture	200,00
10	Sales	80,00	6	Purchases	500,00
17	Rent received	30,00	13	Advertising	50,00

Transaction 11
Remember that John Crossbar owes Bob's Bikes R480. John says that he can only afford to pay R240. Bob accepts the payment and agrees that the balance owing will be left over to the following month.

January 31: Received R240 from John Crossbar in part settlement of his account
This transaction has the effect of decreasing John Crossbar's debt. The asset **John Crossbar** is decreased.

In addition, there is an increase in the bank balance.

Thus, there is both an increase and a decrease in assets. In effect, one asset is being replaced by another.

The bank account is _____ to reflect the receipt of money. John Crossbar's account is _____ to reflect the decrease in debtors.

Put through these entries:

Debit side		BANK ACCOUNT			Credit side	
1997			1997			
Jan 3	Capital	1000,00	Jan 4	Office furniture	200,00
10	Sales	80,00	6	Purchases	500,00
17	Rent received	30,00	13	Advertising	50,00
			27	Rent	80,00
			30	Electricity & water	30,00

Debit side			JOHN CROSSBAR ACCOUNT		Credit side
1997					
Jan 11	Sales	480,00			

Go back over this exercise on Bob's Bikes at least four times. Once you have mastered the concepts dealt with in this chapter, only then move on to the next chapter.

Exercise 4.1

You are the owner of ABC Stores. For each of the following transactions, write down the names of the accounts to be debited and credited in the table supplied.

1. The owner invests R1 000 into the business.
2. Goods bought on credit from JK Suppliers, R300.
3. Paid by cheque for a photocopy machine for office use, R400.
4. Sold goods for cash to D. Goza, R50.
5. Sold goods on credit to J. Richards, R100.
6. Paid for stationery by cheque, R40.
7. Placed an advertisement in *The Tribune*, paid by cheque, R100.
8. Bought goods from RM Suppliers and paid by cheque, R500.
9. Received R100 settlement from debtor, J. Richards.
10. Paid cheque of R250 to the municipality for rates and taxes.
11. Paid R300 to creditor JK Suppliers to settle amount owing.
12. The owner draws R60 from the business for his personal use.

No.	ACCOUNT DEBITED	ACCOUNT CREDITED
1.	Bank	Capital
2.		
3.		
4.		
5.		
6.		
7.		
8.		
9.		
10.		
11.		
12.	Drawings	Bank

20

Test-yourself questions

Question 4.1
Enter the following transactions into the ledger of Sharpes Stationery:

1996
Dec

1	B. Sharpe, the owner, contributes a capital amount of R6 500 to start the business. This amount is deposited into a bank account in the name of the business.
4	Bought a cash register on credit from Willy and Sons for R500.
5	Bought shelving for the shop and paid by cheque, R200.
7	Bought stocks of stationery from Haltons Supplies (Pty) Ltd, and paid by means of cheque, R2 000.
9	Purchased a motor cycle for deliveries from Hobbs Motors on credit for R800.
10	Sold pens and pencils for cash, R50.
13	Fuel for the delivery vehicle cost R10. Paid by cheque.
14	Exercise books and pens sold on credit to Queensmead School for R300.
17	Cash sales R150.
20	Barry Sharpe withdrew R50 from the business for his private use.
23	Paid Hobbs Motors R750 to settle their account, and received a discount of R50.
24	Paid casual wages to delivery driver by cheque, R150.
28	Received R200 on account from Queensmead School.
29	Paid shop rental, R250 by cheque.

Question 4.2
Mr C Brown trading as The Chocolate Shop commenced business on 1 January 1997. The following transactions are to be entered into the ledger of The Chocolate Shop:.

1997
Jan

3	C. Brown, the owner, deposits his capital contribution of R20 000 in a current banking account opened in the name of the firm.
5	Drew a cheque for R150 to pay for a trading licence.
6	Paid for counters and light fittings by cheque, R1 700.
9	Bought goods on credit from Mr Choc for R2 500.
10	Cashed a cheque to pay wages for the week, R250.
13	Bought packing materials from Plastic Supplies and paid by cheque, R400.
16	Sold chocolates for cash, R50.
18	C. Brown cashed a business cheque to pay his personal rates and taxes, R35.
19	Bought stationery on credit from Hearty Stationers for R65.
21	Paid wages, R250.
22	Sold goods on credit to J. Cason, R200.
24	Took a loan from Helpers Bank for R5 000.
25	Paid Mr Choc an amount of R1 500 on account.

28	Paid for a sign to appear outside the shop with the name The Chocolate Shop written on it, R90.
29	Cash sales, R140.
31	Received an amount of R120 on account from J. Cason.

Question 4.3

T. Pegg runs a business called The Music Shop. He buys and sells second-hand musical equipment.

Enter the following transactions into the ledger of The Music Shop:

1996
May

1	T. Pegg increased his capital contribution by bringing his private vehicle into the business at R4 000.
3	Bought 4 guitars at R50 each and paid by cheque.
	Bought 2 keyboards at R370 each and paid by cheque.
4	Bought new furniture on credit from Fine Brothers, R1 000.
7	Paid R50 for repairs to an old chair used in the shop.
10	Fitted and paid cash for an air conditioner to cool the shop, R650.
12	Cash sales, R350.
15	Bought merchandise on credit from Drums Unlimited, R1 300.
19	Sold a keyboard to Joe Bloggs on credit, R550.
23	Cash sales, R750.
24	Paid the garage account, R120, of which R40 was for petrol and the balance for a service.
25	Drew a cheque to pay The Red Cross Society a donation of R75.
26	Bank charges for the month amount to R15.
28	Cash sales, R830.
29	Paid Fine Brothers R300 on account and received their discount for R10.
31	Joe Bloggs paid R300 against his account.

CHAPTER FIVE

The Trial Balance

A. THE LEDGER OF BOB'S BICYCLE SHOP

From Chapter 4, the complete ledger of Bob's Bicycle Shop is shown below:

Debit side			CAPITAL ACCOUNT			Credit side
			1997			
			Jan 3	Bank		1 000,00

			BANK ACCOUNT			
1997			1997			
Jan 3	Capital	1 000,00	Jan 4	Office furniture		200,00
10	Sales	80,00	6	Purchases		500,00
17	Rent received	30,00	13	Advertising		50,00
31	John Crossbar	240,00	27	Rent		80,00
			30	Electricity & water		30,00

			OFFICE FURNITURE ACCOUNT		
1997					
Jan 4	Bank	200,00			

			OFFICE EQUIPMENT ACCOUNT		
1997					
Jan 5	Office Supplies	100,00			

			OFFICE SUPPLIES (PTY) LTD		
			1997		
			Jan 5	Office equipment	100,00

			PURCHASES ACCOUNT		
1997					
Jan 6	Bank	500,00			

			SALES ACCOUNT		
			1997		
			Jan 10	Bank	80,00
			11	John Crossbar	480,00

JOHN CROSSBAR ACCOUNT

1997				1997		
Jan 11	Sales		480,00	Jan 31	Bank	240,00

ADVERTISING ACCOUNT

1997						
Jan 13	Bank		50,00			

RENT RECEIVED ACCOUNT

				1997		
				Jan 17	Bank	30,00

RENT ACCOUNT

1997						
Jan 27	Bank		80,00			

ELECTRICITY AND WATER

1997						
Jan 30	Bank		30,00			

B.   BALANCING LEDGER ACCOUNTS

Some of the ledger accounts above have entries recorded on both the debit and the credit side. These accounts must be balanced in order to show how much is left in the account.

For example, consider the bank account.

Debit side				BANK ACCOUNT		Credit side
1997				1997		
Jan 3	Capital		1 000,00	Jan 4	Office furniture	200,00
10	Sales		80,00	6	Purchases	500,00
17	Rent received		30,00	13	Advertising	50,00
31	John Crossbar		240,00	27	Rent	80,00
				30	Electricity & water	30,00

1.   Add up both sides of the account. Check that the debit side amounts to R1 350 and the credit side to R860.

2.   Now find the difference between the two sides. Do you agree that the difference is R490? This is how much money Bob has left over in the bank at the end of January 1997. This is called the **balance on the bank account**. It is a **debit balance** since the debit side is bigger than the credit side. And we would expect an asset account to have a debit balance.

3.   The bigger total (R1 350) is written under each column of figures on both the debit and the credit side. In order for the credit side to add up to this total, the difference or balance must be written in above the total. This is called the balance **carried down**. The word **Balance** is written in the details column. The abbre-

viation **c/d** (carried down) is written in the folio column. The entry is dated for the last day of the month.

Debit side			BANK ACCOUNT		Credit side	
1997				1997		
Jan 3	Capital	1 000,00	Jan 4	Office furniture		200,00
10	Sales	80,00	6	Purchases		500,00
17	Rent received	30,00	13	Advertising		50,00
31	John Crossbar	240,00	27	Rent		80,00
			30	Electricity & water		30,00
			31	Balance	c/d	490,00
		1 350,00				1 350,00
Feb 1	Balance b/d	490,00				

(Notice that the totals are in line with each other.)

4. Finally, the balance is written on the debit side under the totals. This is called the **balance brought down**. The word **Balance** is written in the details column. The abbreviation **b/d** (brought down) is written in the folio column. This is dated for the first day of the next month (February).

The **balance b/d** shows that there is a debit balance of R490 in the bank account. In other words, R490 is left in the bank on 1 February. Now, go back to the bank account and balance that ledger account on your own.

The only other account that must be balanced is John Crossbar's account. Go through the steps shown above and check that there is a debit balance of R240 on his account. Do this exercise in John Crossbar's ledger account (page 24).

C.   TOTALLING LEDGER ACCOUNTS

An account can have more than one entry on one side only. These accounts need not be balanced; they must be totalled.

For example, the sales account has two entries on the credit side. These amounts are added together and the total of R560 is written below the entries on the credit side. This shows that a total of R560 worth of goods has been sold during January 1997. Do this in the sales account in the ledger (page 23).

D.   THE TRIAL BALANCE

Each transaction is entered into the ledger twice (once as a debit and once as a credit). This means that, at any time, the total of the debit entries must be equal to the total of the credit entries. This is true so long as no errors were made when recording the transactions into the ledger.

In order to test whether the total debits are equal to total credits, we take out a trial balance. This is simply a list of ledger account balances with debit and credit amounts shown in separate columns.

Trial balance of Bob's Bicycle Shop on 31 January 1997

	DEBIT	CREDIT
ASSETS		
Office furniture	200	
Office equipment	100	
Bank	490	
Debtor — John Crossbar	240	
LIABILITIES		
Capital		1 000
Creditor — Office Supplies		100
EXPENSES		
Purchases	500	
Advertising	50	
Rent	80	
Electricity & water	30	
INCOME (REVENUE)		
Sales		560
Rent received		30
	R1 690	R1 690

Since the total of the debit balances is equal to the total of the credit balances, we say that "the trial balance balances".

The trial balance is not part of the accounting process. It is only a check on whether debits and credits have been correctly entered into the ledger.

What happens if the trial balance does not balance?

If the trial balance does not balance, a mistake has been made. You must find the mistake by checking back on the original entries into the ledger accounts.

There are some errors that the trial balance will not identify. Do you see that the following errors will not cause total debits to differ from total credits?

(a) The wrong amount is entered on both the debit and the credit side.
(b) The entry is written into the wrong account.
(c) The transaction is not entered at all.
(d) An identical debit and credit error occurs.

Test-yourself questions

Question 5.1

Go back to Chapter 4. From the ledger for questions 4.1, 4.2 and 4.3 balance and total the accounts and take out a trial balance.

Question 5.2

The following balances were extracted from the books of Joe's Store at 28 February 1996. You are required to group these balances into the form of a trial balance under the following headings:

(a) Assets
(b) Liabilities
(c) Expenses
(d) Income

Then balance the trial balance by inserting the correct bank figure.

	R
Advertising	1 500
Bank	?
Capital	30 000
Debtors	7 500
Drawings	2 300
Discount received	750
Entertainment	1 250
Furniture	9 500
Insurance	2 100
Land and buildings	18 700
Loan from Wonder Bank	10 000
Motor vehicle	8 500
Motor vehicle expenses	1 000
Postage	250
Purchases	29 000
Printing and stationery	300
Sales	44 950
Rent paid	3 100
Creditors	4 300

Question 5.3

Chapman Brothers have an inexperienced bookkeeper who has asked you to help him prepare the trial balance as at 30 April 1996. He provides you with his version of the trial balance which is set out below:

	DEBIT	CREDIT
Capital	5 000	
Bank	850	
Office furniture	1 100	
Drawings		600
Salaries	4 000	
Office equipment		2 500
Purchases	7 000	
Sales		15 000
Discount allowed		200
Bank charges	75	

Advertising	340	
Rent received	860	
Rent	1 780	
Electricity & Water	45	
Debtors		3 200
Creditors	5 700	
Motor vehicle	4 870	
	31 620	21 500

Question 5.4

Arrange the following balances in the form of a trial balance as at 31 December 1996 under the following headings:

(a) Assets
(b) Liabilities
(c) Expenses
(d) Income

Advertising R267; Bank overdraft (overspent and now owe the bank) R1 204; Bad debts R56; Bank charges R62; Commission paid R1 163; Commission received R911; Delivery charges R888; Depreciation R1 226; Electricity R66; Furniture and fittings R2 005; Delivery vehicle R9 500; Delivery vehicle expenses R1 208; Office equipment R1 555; Capital R50 000; Purchases R15 444; Debtors R26 003; Creditors R9 876; Carriage inward R456; Petty cash R250; Sales R29 988; Discount allowed R245; Rent received R1 200; Land and buildings R36 053; Salaries R18 800; Loan from XYZ bank R20 000; Discount received R2 068.

Question 5.5

Indicate the ledger balances which would normally apply in the following cases:

(Note: your answer should state simply: 1 — debit; 2 — credit; 3 — debit; etc)

1. Motor vehicles
2. Capital
3. Drawings
4. Motor vehicle expenses
5. Commission paid
6. Purchases
7. Sales
8. Furniture
9. General expenses
10. Commission received
11. Rent paid
12. Salaries

28

CHAPTER SIX

The Cash Book

A.   INTRODUCTION

The process of Accounting that has been outlined so far can be summarised as follows:

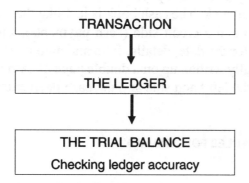

Business transactions are entered into the ledger. At the end of a month, ledger accounts are balanced and totalled. A trial balance is then taken out showing each ledger account balance.

Make sure that you understand this process and that you have done all the exercises in the previous chapters.

B.   THE CASH BOOK

Go back to the beginning of Chapter 5 and look at the ledger accounts. Do you see that the bank account contains many more entries than the other accounts? Since most businesses have many cash transactions, the bank account is usually quite busy.

Because the bank account contains so many entries, we are going to move the bank account to its own separate book (called the **cash book**). Now, instead of entering cash transactions into the bank account in the ledger, we will enter them into the cash book. Don't let this confuse you. Simply remember that the bank account is now in a separate book called the cash book.

The cash book is divided into two sections:

1.   The cash receipts section — keeps track of money received by the business.
2.   The cash payments section — keeps track of money paid out by the business.

In its most basic form, the **cash receipts** section of the cash book looks as follows:

CASH RECEIPTS BOB'S BIKES FOR JANUARY 1997

Doc	Day	Details	Fol	Bank

In its most basic form, the **cash payments** section of the cash book looks as follows:

CASH PAYMENTS BOB'S BIKES FOR JANUARY 1997

Cheque	Day	Details	Fol	Bank

If we place the cash receipts and cash payments sections of the cash book alongside each other, we have a cash book. The cash book is just like the bank account. It has a debit side (cash receipts) and a credit side (cash payments). Like any other ledger account, it has a column for the date, details, folio and amount (bank).

The cash book is usually written up on a double page of cash book paper, with the cash receipts section on the left hand side and the cash payments section on the right hand side.

CASH BOOK OF BOB'S BICYCLES FOR JANUARY 1997

CASH RECEIPTS   CASH PAYMENTS

Doc	Day	Details	Fol	Bank	Cheq	Day	Details	Fol	Bank

Exercise 6.1

The bank account of Bob's bicycle shop appears below. Rewrite the contents of this account into the cash book of Bob's Bicycles. You may ignore the "document", "folio" and "cheque" columns for the moment.

Debit side		BANK ACCOUNT			Credit side
1997			1997		
Jan 3	Capital	1 000,00	Jan 4	Office furniture	200,00
10	Sales	80,00	6	Purchases	500,00
17	Rent received	30,00	13	Advertising	50,00
31	John Crossbar	240,00	27	Rent	80,00
			30	Electricity & water	30,00

CASH BOOK OF BOB'S BICYCLES FOR JANUARY 1997

CASH RECEIPTS   CASH PAYMENTS

Doc	Date	Details	Fol	Bank	Cheq	Date	Details	Fol	Bank

30

Do you see that a bank account and a cash book are the same thing ?

C.   THE CASH RECEIPTS SECTION OF THE CASH BOOK

The Cash Receipts section is really just the debit side of the cash book.

The Cash Receipts section of the cash book is used to record all money coming into the business. This includes:

1.   Cash paid into the business by the owner as capital.
2.   Sale of goods for cash.
3.   Payment received from debtors.
4.   Receipt of income sources other than sales, for example, rent received.

All the above transactions have one thing in common. They all increase the amount of money in the business bank account.

We will now add a few columns to the Cash Receipts section of the cash book. The reason for this will become clear later on. The expanded Cash Receipts section is laid out as follows:

CASH BOOK OF _____ FOR JUNE 1996

CASH RECEIPTS

Doc	Date	Details	Folio	Sundries	Sales	Debtors	Bank

The sales column is used to record all **sales of goods for cash**.

The debtors' column is used to record all **payments received from debtors**.

The sundries column is used to record any **other receipt of money**.

IN ADDITION TO WRITING THE AMOUNT RECEIVED IN THE ANALYSIS COLUMNS MENTIONED ABOVE, THE AMOUNT IS ALSO WRITTEN IN THE BANK COLUMN.

Example 6.1

The following transactions are to be entered into the books of ALLICATS (PTY) LTD, a clothing store.

Some of the balances in the ledger of Allicats (Pty) Ltd at 1 June 1996 are as follows:

B. Skidrow (debtor)   R200
A. Taylor   (debtor)   R300

1996
June

2	Allan Catson, the owner, increases his capital by R1 000
5	Cash sales, R150.
8	B. Skidrow pays R80 on account.
19	Sold goods to M. Brookes for cash, R240.
29	A. Taylor pays R250 against his account of R300.

Before you write up the cash book, you should analyse each transaction to decide what account must be debited and what account must be credited.

Date of entry	A/c debited	A/c credited
June 2	Bank (cash book)	Capital
June 5	Bank (cash book)	Sales
June 8	Bank (cash book)	B. Skidrow
June 19	Bank (cash book)	Sales*
June 29	Bank (cash book)	A. Taylor

* Remember that when goods are sold for cash the name of the buyer is not recorded.

The common feature among the above transactions is that they all increase the amount of money in the bank. Therefore, each entry is debited to the cash book (bank account).

The debit side of the cash book (cash receipts section) would look as follows:

CASH BOOK OF ALLICATS FOR JUNE 1996

CASH RECEIPTS   CB1

Doc	Date	Details	Folio	Sundries	Sales	Debtors	Bank
BDS	2	CAPITAL		1 000			1 000
CSS	5	SALES			150		150
REC	8	B. SKIDROW				80	80
CSS	19	SALES			240		240
REC	29	A. TAYLOR				250	250
				1 000	390	330	1 720

The page reference number
The reference number on the top right hand corner is CB1 indicating that this is the first page in the cash book. The second page would be CB2 and so on.

The document column
The abbreviations in the document column stand for the following:

BDS — Bank deposit slip. Issued by the bank on deposit of money.
CSS — Cash sales slip. This is given to a customer who pays cash.
REC — Receipt. This is given to a debtor who pays his or her account.

The sales and debtors' columns
At the end of the month, the sales and debtors' columns are totalled. You can see that cash sales totalled R390 for the month. In addition, debtors paid a total of R330.

The bank column
The total in the bank column is the total amount of money received into the bank. It is the total debit entry to the bank account.

Posting to the credit accounts

Although the debits have all been put into the cash book, there are no credit entries yet. We still have to put through the credit entries into the capital account, the sales account and the debtors' accounts. We say that we "post" to these accounts.

1. The capital account must be credited with R1 000.

CAPITAL ACCOUNT — 1

1996			
June 2	Bank	CB 1	1 000,00

Notice that the folio column contains a reference to where the information was posted from. It tells you that the debit entry is in the cash book, page 1. At the same time the folio column in the cash book shows that the R1 000 was posted to ledger account number 1 (L1).

2. The sales account must be credited with R150 and R240. But we can save time here by posting one total of R390 instead of two separate amounts. The sales total will be posted to the sales account (assume that it is account number 23) in the ledger as follows:

SALES ACCOUNT — 23

1996			
Jun 30	Bank	CB 1	390,00

Notice that the entry is dated 30 June. This is because the entry is posted at the end of the month since it is the total sales figure for the month of June.

Once again, the debit entry is in the cash book. A folio reference is written in the cash book under the sales total to show that the sales amount of R390 has been posted.

3. The debtors' accounts must now be credited. We must credit each debtor's account separately since we have to keep a separate record of how much each individual debtor owes us. This means that Skidrow must be credited with R150 and Taylor must be credited with R240.

B. SKIDROW — 16

1996				1996			
Jun 1	Balance	b/d	200,00	Jun 8	Bank	CB 1	80,00

A. TAYLOR — 17

1996				1996			
Jun 1	Balance	b/d	300,00	Jun 29	Bank	CB 1	250,00

The debtors' balances that were given at the beginning of this example are shown on the debit side of the accounts. Since debtors are assets, they must have debit balances.

The credit entries are posted from the cash book, page 1 (CB1). Each debtor is credited with the amount that he has paid. A reference is made in the folio column in the cash book that the amounts have been posted to L16 and L17.

Once the postings have all been put through, the cash book now looks as follows:

CASH RECEIPTS SECTION OF ALLICATS FOR JUNE 1996   **CB 1**

Doc	Date	Details	Folio	Sundries	Sales	Debtors	Bank
BDS	2	CAPITAL	L1	1 000			1 000
CSS	5	SALES	✓		150		150
REC	8	B. SKIDROW	L16			80	80
CSS	19	SALES	✓		240		240
REC	29	A. TAYLOR	L17			250	250
				1 000	390	330	1 720

L23

The principle of equal debits and credits still applies. If you add up the debit entries in the cash book, they total R1 720. Now add up the credit postings. Do you see that they also total R1 720?

Notice that the folio reference to L23 is written under the sales total. This is because the amounts were not posted separately but as a total.

D.   DISCOUNT ALLOWED TO DEBTORS

We may offer debtors a settlement discount if they pay us within a specified period. For example, debtors may be offered a 2% discount for payment within 30 days of purchase. This is called **discount allowed** and it is an expense to the business that offers the discount.

Discount allowed is entered into a separate column (the discount allowed column) in the Cash Receipts section of the Cash Book.

Example 6.2
Enter the following information into the cash book of Jolly Stores for March 1996:

March 1   Received payment of R380 from a debtor, K. Zondo and allowed a discount of R20. Issued receipt no. 10.

March 5   J. Bona paid R300 and was allowed a discount of 5% on this amount.

March 8   M. Cawood owes R500. He settles this amount by means of a payment of R475.

March 9   B. Carter owes R200. He pays this amount less 2,5% discount.

34

CASH BOOK OF JOLLY STORES FOR MARCH 1996

CASH RECEIPTS

Doc	Date	Details	Fol	Sundry	Sales	Debtors	Disc allowed	Bank
R10	1	K. Zondo				400	20	380
R11	5	J. Bona				315	15	300
R12	8	M . Cawood				500	25	475
R13	9	B. Carter				200	5	195

Note that the discount allowed is added to the payment from the debtor and the total is shown in the Debtors' column. This is because the debt from the debtor is to be reduced by the amount of the payment and by the discount allowed to him.

In the case of K. Zondo on 1 March 1996, the double entry is as follows:

Debit   Bank   R380
Debit   Discount allowed   R 20
                Credit K. Zondo   R400

Note that the total debit of R400 is equal to the total credit of R400.

Since discount allowed is an expense account, it stands to reason that it should be debited in the ledger. Once the cash book is closed at the end of the month, the discount allowed column is added up. This total is posted to the debit side of the discount allowed account.

Exercise 6.2
Complete the ledger of Jolly Stores by posting the rest of the entries in the receipts section of the cash book. (Note that there would normally be debit balances on the debtors' accounts.)

K. ZONDO

	1996			
	Mar 1	Bank & discount	CB1	400,00

J. BONA

M. CAWOOD

B. CARTER

Exercise 6.3

Enter the following transactions into the Cash Receipts section of the cash book of Skylight Jewellers for May 1996. The list of debtors' balances on 1 May 1996 appears below:

Mrs C. Ruby	R450,00
Mr J. Radebe	R300,00
Mrs K. Johnstone	R600,00

At the end of May 1996, close off the cash book and post to the correct ledger accounts.

1996
May

4   Goods sold for cash, R270.
8   Received R180 on account from Mr Radebe.
9   Received commission from Gem Supplies, R500.
15   Mrs Ruby paid off her account in full and was allowed a discount of 5%.
19   The owner increased his capital contribution by R3 000.
25   Diamond bracelet sold to G. Digger for cash, R375.
28   Mrs Johnstone paid off R450 on her account and received a discount of R10.

Exercise 6.4

Select the appropriate transactions and enter them into the Cash Receipts section of the cash book for Monty's Hardware Store for January 1997. At the end of the month, post to the relevant ledger accounts:

1977
Jan

1   Monty, the owner, contributes additional capital by depositing R5 000 into the business bank account.
5   Cash sales, R750.
9   Joe Citizen, a debtor owing R600, pays R350 on account and is allowed a discount of R30.
14   Sold goods on credit to K. Harris for R300 and for cash to J. Bean for R800.
19   Rent received from ABC Stores rental of a section of the storeroom, R550.
24   Cash sales, R370.
27   B. Zuma, a debtor owing R950, pays 50% of what he owes and is allowed a discount of R40.
29   Bought goods on credit from JK Wholesalers for R5 000.

CHAPTER SEVEN

The Cash Book — Continued

A. INTRODUCTION

In the previous chapter, we looked at the debit side of the cash book. In this chapter, we discuss the credit side of the cash book, known as the cash payments section of the cash book.

B. THE CASH PAYMENTS SECTION OF THE CASH BOOK

The cash payments section of the cash book is simply another term for the credit side of the cash book. The following types of transactions are typically entered on the credit side of the cashbook:

1.   Cash payment for an asset.
2.   Cash payment for a business expense.
3.   Cash payment to a creditor.
4.   Cash payment for goods (purchases).

Take note that a cash payment means payment by means of cheque. Most businesses have bank accounts and they make payments by cheque.

The cash payments section of the cash book is set out as follows:

CASH BOOK OF _____ FOR JUNE 1996

CASH PAYMENTS

Doc	Date	Details	Fol	Sundries	Purchases	Creditors	Bank

The Purchases column records all **cash purchases of goods**.

The Creditors column records all **payments to creditors**.

The Sundries column records all **other cash payments**.

ALL PAYMENTS ARE SHOWN IN ONE OF THE ABOVE ANALYSIS COLUMNS AS WELL AS IN THE BANK COLUMN.

Example 7.1

On 1 June 1996 a clothing shop called Allicats had the following creditors:

Fashion Outfitters	R1 000
Impress Dress	R 850

Enter the transactions below into the cashbook of Allicats for the month of June 1996.

1996
June
4   Paid for advertising space in *Fair Style* magazine, R120. Paid by cheque 001.
8   Sent a cheque to Fashion Outfitters for R300.
13   Bought a new range of dresses and paid by cheque, R890
14   Paid the telephone account, R50.
21   Cash payment to Impress Dress, R500.
27   Goods bought for cash, R450.
30   Bank charges for the month amount to R10.

Before you write up the cash book, you should analyse each transaction to decide what account must be debited and what account must be credited.

Date of entry	A/c debited	A/c credited
June 4	Advertising	Bank (cash book)
June 8	Fashion Outfitters	Bank (cash book)
June 13	Purchases	Bank (cash book)
June 14	Telephone	Bank (cash book)
June 21	Impress Dress	Bank (cash book)
June 27	Purchases	Bank (cash book)
June 30	Bank charges	Bank (cash book)

The common feature among these transactions is that they all **decrease** the amount of money in the bank. Therefore, each entry is credited to the cash book (bank account).

   The cash payment section of the cash book is written up as follows:

CASH BOOK OF ALLICATS FOR JUNE 1996

CASH PAYMENTS   CB 1

Cheq	Date	Details	Fol	Sundries	Purchases	Creditors	Bank
001	4	Advertising	L11	120			120
002	8	Fashion Out.	L14			300	300
003	13	Purchases	✓		890		890
004	14	Telephone	L12	50			50
005	21	Impress Dr.	L15			500	500
006	27	Purchases	✓	10	450		450
B/S	30	Bank Charg.	L13				10
				180	1 340	800	2 320

L20

The page reference number

The reference number on the top right hand corner is CB1 indicating that this is the first page in the cash book.

The document column

Since payments are made by cheque, the document is always the cheque counterfoil. The number of the cheque (which is shown on the counterfoil) is used as a reference. Bank charges are deducted directly from your account by the bank and the document that informs you of this is the bank statement (B/S).

The purchases and creditors' columns

At the end of the month, the purchases and creditors' columns are totalled. Notice that cash purchases totals R1 340 for the month. In addition, creditors were paid a total of R800.

The bank column

Remember that the cash book is also the ledger account for Bank. Any transaction entered into the Cash Payments section of the cash book is a credit in the bank account.

Posting to the debit accounts

From the payments section of the cash book, we only post the debit amount to the ledger. The names of the accounts written in the details column of the cash payments section are now debited in the ledger. Let's begin with posting the Sundries column. The first account in that column is the advertising account.

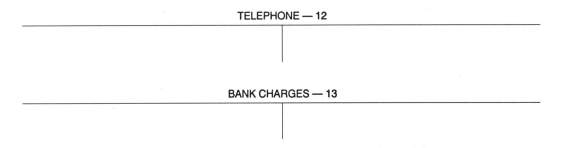

ADVERTISING — 11

1996				
June 4	Bank	CB1	120,00	

Notice that the folio column in the advertising account contains a reference to where the information was posted from. It tells you that the credit entry is in the cash book, page 1. At the same time the folio column in the cash book shows that the R120 was posted to ledger account number 11 (L11).

Now, you put through the debit entries to the telephone and bank charges accounts below:

TELEPHONE — 12

BANK CHARGES — 13

The purchases account must be debited with R890 and R450. Again, we can save time here by posting one total of R1 340 instead of two separate amounts. The purchases total will be posted to the purchases account (assume that it is account number 20) in the ledger as follows:

PURCHASES ACCOUNT — 20

1996				
June 30	Bank	CB1	1 340,00	

The folio CB1 tells us that the entry was posted from the cash book, page 1. The folio reference under the Purchases column in the cash book indicates that the R1 340 was posted to account number 20 in the general ledger (L20).

Once again, the entry is dated 30 June. It is posted at the end of the month since it is the total purchases for the month of June.

The creditors' accounts must now be debited. We debit each creditors' account separately since we have to keep a separate record of how much is owed to each individual creditor. This means that Fashion Outfitters is debited with R300 and Impress Dress is debited with R500.

FASHION OUTFITTERS — 14

1996				1996			
Jun 8	Bank	CB1	300,00	Jun 1	Balance	b/d	1 000,00

IMPRESS DRESS — 15

1996				1996			
Jun 21	Bank	CB1	500,00	Jun 1	Balance	b/d	850,00

The balances that were given at the beginning of this example are shown on the credit side of the accounts. As you know, creditors are liabilities with credit balances.

The debit entries are posted from the cash book, page 1. Each creditor is debited with the amount that was paid to him. A reference is made in the folio column in the cash book that the amounts have been posted to L14 and L15.

Once the postings have all been put through, the cash payments section of the cash book looks as follows:

CASH BOOK OF ALLICATS FOR JUNE 1996

CASH PAYMENTS   CB 1

Cheq	Date	Details	Fol	Sundries	Purchases	Creditors	Bank
001	4	Advertising	L11	120			120
002	8	Fashion Out.	L14			300	300
003	13	Purchases	✓		890		890
004	14	Telephone	L12	50			50
005	21	Impress Dress	L15			500	500
006	27	Purchases	✓		450		450
B\S	30	Bank Charges	L13	10			10
				180	1 340	800	2 320

L20

40

There is a credit total of R2 320 in the bank column of the cash payments section of the cash book. We have posted debits also totalling R2 320 made up as follows:

Advertising	120
Telephone	50
Bank charges	10
Purchases	1 340
Fashion Outfitters	300
Impress Dress	500
Total	R2 320

Therefore, the total credits in the ledger are equal to the total debits.

Exercise 7.1
Enter the following transactions into the cash payments section of the cash book of **The Music Man,** a retailer of musical instruments.

On 1 August the following creditors' balances appear in the ledger:

Instrument Supplies	R1 500
Guitars Unlimited	R2 000
Musical Matters	R1 000

1996
August

4	Drew cheque number 050 to pay Guitars Unlimited on account R1 200.
6	Bought a calculator for the office and paid R85 by cheque.
9	Cash purchases, R2 500.
14	Paid R100 for rates and taxes for the shop premises.
17	Paid R600 on account to Musical Matters.
22	The owner paid his personal insurance policy by means of cheque 055, R30.
23	Bought two saxophones from The Sax Shop and paid R400.
26	Drew a cheque to pay R1 000 on account to Instrument Supplies.
30	Bought an air-conditioner from Aircon Services and paid by cheque, R1 200.

Close off the cash book and post to the relevant ledger accounts.

C. DISCOUNT RECEIVED FROM CREDITORS

When payments are made to creditors within a specified period, we may receive a cash discount. This is called a **discount received**. For example, we may receive a 2% discount from a creditor if payment is made within 30 days of purchase.

Discount received is entered into a separate column (the discount received column) in the Cash Payments section of the cash book.

Example 7.2

Enter the following information into the cash book of Nellie Traders for May 1996.

May

1	Paid Hope Stores (Pty) Ltd R1 000 by cheque number 18 and received a discount of R80.
6	Paid R1 200 to Mills Clothing and received their discount of 5% on the amount paid.
9	Owed R800 to Rapp Stores. Settled this amount by means of a payment of R780.
10	Owed R600 to Joy Trading. Paid this amount less 2,5% discount.

CASH BOOK OF NELLIE TRADERS FOR MAY 1996

CASH PAYMENTS

Cheq	Date	Details	Fol	Sundry	Purch	Credi-tors	Disc rec'd	Bank
18	1	Hope Stores				1 080	80	1 000
19	6	Mills Clothing				1 260	60	1 200
20	9	Rapp Stores				800	20	780
21	10	Joy Trading				600	15	585
							175	

Note that the discount received is added to the bank amount and this total is shown in the Creditors' column. This is because our debt to the creditor is to be reduced by the amount of the payment plus the discount received from the creditor.

In the case of Hope Stores on 1 May 1996, the double entry is as follows:

Debit Hope Stores   R1 080

                          Credit Bank   R1 000
                          Credit Discount Received   R   80

Since discount received is an income account, it stands to reason that it should be credited in the ledger. Once the cash book is closed at the end of the month, the Discount Received column is added up. This total (R175) is posted to the **credit** side of the **Discount Received** account.

Exercise 7.2

Complete the ledger of Nellie Traders by posting the rest of the entries in the cash payments journal. (Note that there would normally be credit balances on the creditors' accounts.)

HOPE STORES

1996	
May 1 Bank & Discount CB1 1 080,00	

MILLS CLOTHING

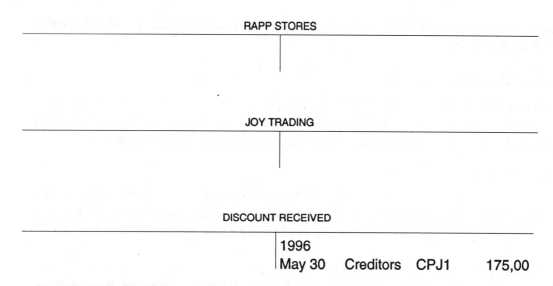

RAPP STORES
_____|_____

JOY TRADING
_____|_____

DISCOUNT RECEIVED
_____|_____
                              | 1996
                              | May 30   Creditors   CPJ1   175,00

Check that the total debits in the creditors' accounts are equal to the total credits in the bank and discount received accounts.

D. THE BANK BALANCE

If the bank balance is **favourable** (there is money in the bank), then the balance is brought down in the Cash Receipts section of the cash book. This is a debit balance that shows money in the bank as an asset.

If the bank balance is **unfavourable**, (the bank is overdrawn), then the balance is brought down in the Cash Payments section of the cash book. This is a credit balance that shows that money is owed to the bank and is therefore a liability. It is known as a bank overdraft.

E. R/D CHEQUES, CANCELLED CHEQUES AND DIRECT DEPOSITS

R/D cheques

We may receive a cheque that is later returned by the bank marked R/D **(Refer to drawer)**. The drawer of the cheque has insufficient funds to honour the cheque. We say that the cheque has been dishonoured. We must contact the drawer to rectify the situation.

When it was first deposited, the cheque was entered into the Receipts section of the cash book. Now that we know it is dishonoured, the entry must be **reversed out** by means of an entry in the Payments section of the cash book. Whatever was written in the details column of the Receipts section is also written in the details column of the Payments section. This cancels out the original entry.

If the R/D cheque was received from a debtor, then the name of the debtor should be written in the Payments section to reverse the entry. However, because there is no **Debtors' column** in the Payments section, you should show this entry in the **Sundries column**.

Cancelled cheques

If we write out a cheque that is cancelled after it has been entered in the Payments section of the cash book, it must be reversed by means of an entry in the Receipts

43

section. Be sure to show the same description in the details column so that the entry is fully reversed.

Direct deposits

When a debtor pays directly into our bank account, this is called a direct deposit. Once we receive the bank statement, we can confirm that the money has been put into our account. Then we enter this receipt into the Receipts section of the cash book.

Exercise 7.3

Write up the cash book of WELLOFF & COMPANY for March 1996 using the following information. Use a double piece of cash book paper to and show the Cash Receipts section on the left and the Cash Payments section on the right hand side of the page.

Opening balances/totals on 1 March:
Bank balance R1102,20 (overdraft); Cash sales R106,60; Receipts from debtors R14260,20; Discount allowed R106,60; Paid rent R1000,00; Paid wages R150,00.

Mar
3   Receipts from debtors R11002,10; Discount allowed R49,20; Paid creditors R4620,00; Discount received R96,50; Paid telephone R266,40; Cash sales R642,10.
9   Paid insurance R560,00; Paid garage petrol account R488,80; Receipts from debtors R5027,00.
14   Paid wages R260,10; Bought furniture R1500,00 cash and received a discount of R150,00.
20   Bank charges debited R26,60; Interest on overdraft R106,65; Bought stock R9200,70; Paid rates R860,00.
26   Insurance stop order paid R1200,00; Received from debtors R4045,60; Cash sales R267,70; Paid salary of Mr A R500,25 and salary of Mr B R688,60.
31   Paid PAYE tax R148,00; The owner draws money for his own use R300,00; Received from debtors R1087,40; Cash sales R402,60; Paid creditors R4698,10; Received advice from bankers that an amount of R300 was paid directly into the bank by a debtor.

You are required to balance the cash book.

Exercise 7.4

The owner of Cepp Printing has kept the following basic records of his daily cash transactions. He has asked you to properly record this information in a cash book. All payments are made by cheque. Finally, post to the relevant ledger accounts.

1992
Apr
1   Started the business with R1 925 and deposited it into the bank.
2   Paid rent for the month, R700 (cheque 759).
     Bought goods for R750 on credit.
     Sold some goods for R735. R450 of this amount was to debtors on account and the rest was cash sales.

44

3   Received R24 500 from debtors and allowed a discount of R165.
      Purchased a new receptionist's desk for R1 850 and was allowed a 5% discount for prompt payment (cheque 760).
      Bought stationery for R56 (cheque 761).

5   Paid casual wages, R200 (cheque 762).

14   Bought goods for R5 405 and paid by cheque.
      Banked cash sales for the week, R882.

15   The owner took R400 for his own use.
      Paid creditors accounts of R1 200 and was allowed a discount of $2\frac{1}{2}\%$.

17   Received advice from the bank that a cheque for R265 from R. Morton which was banked as cash sales had been dishonoured.
      Paid fire insurance premiums of R250 (cheque 766).

18   Paid motor vehicles repairs account, R316.
      Received R956 from debtors after allowing discount of R44.

20   Paid electricity and water account for R181.
      Made a donation to Operation Hunger for R125.

21   Banked cash sales of R4 150.
      The insurance company returned the cheque issued on 17 April (cheque 766) advising that the premium is in fact R520 and requesting a replacement cheque (cheque 770).

23   Bought goods for cash, R7 272 (cheque 771).

25   Paid monthly salary to receptionist Ms Gosa for R1 850.
      Paid monthly salary to G. Khumalo, R1 350.
      Paid cheque 774 to PQR Stationers for R1 750 for goods purchased. This amount is made up of R1 630 for the company and R120 worth of private goods for the owner.

28   Banked cash sales of R3 780.

30   The bank has informed you of service charges of R31.

You are required to draw up and balance the cash book for the month of April. All calculations must be made to the nearest rand. You must use three-column cash book paper.

Exercise 7.5

Craig Fulton, a retail Windsurfer merchant, banks all receipts daily and makes all payments by cheque. At the start of the month, Craig Fulton had an overdraft of R3 456,00. You are required to draw up a cash book for the month of March 1996 and post to the relevant ledger accounts.

1996
Mar

2   Purchased from Helen's Sails goods worth R10 450 and paid by cheque 521 after allowing for a 5% discount.
      Cash sales for the week (slips 5432 – 5529) — R7 600
      Received R5 000 from L. Pollard which is the net amount owing from him after allowing 7,5% discount.

9   Paid Carolyn Estates R4 500 for March's rent by credit transfer into their account.

Received R10 000 from Craig Fulton as an additional capital contribution.

Banked cash sales for the week (slips 5530 – 5987) — R5 430

Paid R50 to petty cash with cheque 522.

Paid R7 500 for a new delivery vehicle with a deposit of 30% of the sale price with cheque 532.

Collected R359 from Main Road Cycles and banked it.

Cash sales for the week (slips 5988 – 6543) — R3 767

Paid telephone bill for February, R85 (Cheque 524)

Paid City Treasurer for rates and taxes (R125) and electricity and water (R307).

23   Paid R15 for postage stamps

Paid R5 900 with cheque 527 to Ferndale Clothing for goods for resale.

Cash sales (slips 6544 – 6987) — R10 003

Received R675 from Louise Sports in settlement of their debt of R708.

30   Cash sales (slips 6988 – 7096) — R9 226

Bank statements indicate that there are bank charges of R63 and interest received of R29 for March 1996.

Received and banked the following amounts from debtors:

IS Management Sports	R56
MSI Commercial Cyclists	R89
Anthea's Bikes	R92

Paid salaries as follows:

C. Fulton (cheque 528)	R3 000
C. Smith (cheque 529)	R1 800
B. London (cheque 530)	R1 682

Paid for goods from Durban Surf 'n Sail with cheque 531 for R17 563.

Exercise 7.6

Glenda de Villiers carries on a business as a retail chemist in a new Gauteng shopping centre. She keeps her accounting records as simple as possible and only has a ledger, journal and cash book. Her cash book is a three-column one ruled for cash, bank and discount, and has, up to now, been completed by her bookkeeper, Janine Lee, who has now gone off on maternity leave. Glenda approaches you for help and gives you the following information:

The balances reflected on Janine's last trial balance, at 30 September 1995 were:

Cash on hand	R 120
Cash in the bank	R2 160

The following transactions were entered into during October 1995:

Sent a cheque to Main Property Administrators for R1 500 for the rental of shop space (R1 400) for October 1995 and water and electricity (R100) for September 1995.

Purchased on credit from Mahmood Soaps and Toiletries (Pty) Ltd:

200 cans men's deodorants at R2,75 per can. These are marked up by 150%.

Bottles of moisturising creams at R425, which were net of a trade discount of 15%.

46

Paid to Dobson Druggists a cheque for R375 for a shop display unit for their new range of vitamin supplements.

Cash sales received for the first week of October (to Friday 6 October) were:

For prescription medicines, R12 123

For over-the-counter pills, toiletries, baby items etc, R4 564

For luxury perfumes, R3 766

Paid Patrick, a casual worker, his weekly wage of R150.

Banked all but R100 of the cash.

Paid Glenda's personal butcher's account with a cheque for R56.

Paid R540 by cheque to Hipzopur Contraceptives in full settlement of R600 worth of merchandise purchased in August 1995.

Paid R50 for stamps.

Cash sales received for the second week of October (to Friday 13 October) were:

For prescription medicines, R10 985

For over-the-counter pills, toiletries, baby items etc, R6 664

For luxury perfumes, R2 750

Paid Patrick, a casual worker, his weekly wage of R150.

Banked all but R100 of the cash.

Cash sales received for the third week of October (to Friday 20 October) were:

For prescription medicines, R8 946

For over-the-counter pills, toiletries, baby items, R8 453

Banked all but R100 of the cash

A customer, who was allowed credit, paid off R100 of his R250 account. The rest has been promised in the first week of November.

Paid salary cheques for October to the staff as follows:

Sean   R1 500

Jonah   R1 800

Mark   R1 800

Cash sales received for the fourth week of October (to Friday 27 October) were:

For prescription medicines, R3 211

For over-the-counter pills, toiletries, baby items etc, R15 976

For luxury perfumes, R2 500

Banked all but R250 of the cash.

Paid Mahmood Soaps and Toiletries what was owing to them and claimed a settlement discount of 5%.

You are required to prepare Glenda's cash book for October 1995.

Note that this exercise requires that you use a "cash" as well as a "bank" column in the Receipts section of the cash book. The cash column is used to record money as it is received. When the money is banked, the total deposit is shown in the bank column.

CHAPTER EIGHT

The Petty Cash Book

A. INTRODUCTION

Businesses pay out large amounts of money by cheque. However, there are times when a small amount of money must be paid out. For example, money may be needed to buy postage stamps or office teas. It does not make sense to make such small payments by cheque. For this reason, most businesses keep a small amount of cash called PETTY CASH.

The petty cash is locked up in the PETTY CASH BOX. One staff member is given the job of keeping control of the petty cash. This person is called the petty cashier.

If any member of staff wants money from petty cash, he or she must complete a PETTY CASH VOUCHER. The voucher is a request for petty cash and must be authorised by a manager. The petty cash voucher is handed in to the petty cashier in exchange for cash.

The petty cash voucher looks like this:

```
┌─────────────────────────────────────────────┐
│            Voucher number 235                 │
│                                               │
│                                               │
│          Date _____                      │
│                                               │
│  Details of payment _____  │
│                                               │
│                                               │
│  _____  │
│                                               │
│  _____  │
│                                               │
│  Authorised by _____  │
│                                               │
│  Signature _____  │
│                                               │
└─────────────────────────────────────────────┘
```

B. THE IMPREST SYSTEM

Most business run their petty cash on the imprest system. At the beginning of each month, a specified amount of money (the imprest amount) is put into the petty cash box.

For example, at ABC Ltd, the imprest amount is R100. On the first day of the month, R100 cash is placed into the petty cash box. In return for properly authorised vouchers, the petty cashier pays out cash from the petty cash box. For example, a voucher for R5 for postage stamps is received. The petty cashier takes the voucher and pays out R5 from the box. The petty cash box now contains R95 cash and a voucher for R5. This is still a total of R100.

Another voucher for R15 is received. The petty cashier pays out the cash and puts the voucher in the petty cash box. The box now contains R80 cash and R20 in vouchers. This is still a total of R100 (the imprest amount). At any time, the cash plus the vouchers in the petty cash box must total R100.

Assume that at the end of the month, the box contains R7 cash and R93 in vouchers. Under the imprest system, a cheque is cashed at the bank to REPLACE THE MONEY SPENT DURING THE MONTH. In this case, a cheque for R93 is cashed. This is added to the existing R7 to restore the imprest amount of R100. Therefore on the first day of the following month, there is once again R100 cash in the petty cash box.

The imprest amount is not only replaced at the end of the month. The petty cash can be "topped up" at any time during the month if the petty cash is running short. The same principle applies at any time — REPLACE THE AMOUNT OF MONEY THAT HAS BEEN SPENT SO FAR.

C.   THE PETTY CASH BOOK

The set-out of the petty cash book is as follows:

Debit side   Credit side   PCB1

Day	Details	Amount	Day	Details	Vouch No.	Total	Post	Statio- nery	Sun- dry

The petty cash book is the **ledger account for petty cash**. There is a debit side and a credit side. Since petty cash is an asset, a debit entry is a receipt of money into petty cash (more petty cash). A credit entry is a payment from petty cash (less petty cash).

The debit side of the petty cash book
The debit side of the petty cash book consists of only three columns:

1.   Day
2.   Details
3.   Amount

Whenever a cheque is cashed and the money put into the petty cash box, the petty cash book is debited. The other part of the transaction is a credit to the cash book (since money has been paid out from the bank).

Whenever a cheque is cashed for petty cash, the word **bank** must be written in the details column along with the date and the amount.

The credit side of the petty cash book
Any payments from petty cash are entered on the credit side of the petty cash book. The following columns are provided:

1.   Day
The day on which the transaction took place is written in this column.

2. **Details**
   Write in the details of the payment from petty cash in this column.
3. **Voucher number**
   The number of the petty cash voucher is written in this column.
4. **Total**
   The amount for every payment is written in this column.
5. **Analysis columns**
   The example given uses **postage** and **stationery** as analysis columns. The amount spent on either of these items is written into the appropriate column. However, columns should be used for any REGULAR payment from petty cash. In most exercises, you will be told which columns to use.
6. **The sundry column**
   The sundry column is used to record any payment for which there is no analysis column. In the example given, any payment other than postage and stationery is written into the sundry column.

Example 8.1

Bona Electrical keeps a columnar petty cash book based on the imprest system. The imprest amount is R150. Use columns for postage and stationery. Write up the following petty cash transactions and balance off the petty cash book at 31 March 1996:

1996
Mar

1	Petty cash on hand	R150
4	Bought postage stamps (voucher 1)	R15
8	Bought cleaning materials	R23
11	Bought pens and pencils	R11
15	Paid casual wages	R45
17	Paid for envelopes and invoice books	R27
24	Donation to Operation Hunger	R10
27	Bought postage stamps	R8
31	Restore the imprest amount	

Writing up the petty cash book

The set-out of the petty cash book is as follows:

PETTY CASH BOOK OF BONA ELECTRICAL FOR MARCH 1996

Debit side   Credit side   PCB1

Day	Details	Amount	Day	Details	Vouch	Total	Post	Stat	Sund
1	Balance	R150	4	Stamps	1	15	15		
			8	Clean	2	23			23
			11	Stat	3	11		11	
			15	Wages	4	45			45
			17	Stat	5	27		27	
			24	Donat	6	10			10
			27	Post	7	8	8		

Note that:

1. The voucher numbers are in sequence.
2. ALL payments are entered into the TOTAL column.
3. The last entry on 31 March is dealt with in the next section.

Balancing the petty cash book

The petty cash book is balanced as follows:

1. Add up the total column, the analysis columns (postage and stationery) and the sundry column.
2. Check that the total of the POSTAGE, STATIONERY and SUNDRIES columns equals the total of the TOTAL column.
3. The TOTAL column shows that R139 was spent during the month of March. According to the imprest system, this amount must now be replaced. Therefore on 31 March a cheque is cashed for R139 and this money is put into petty cash.
4. Now balance the petty cash book in the same way that you would balance the cash book or any ledger account. Since there is debit total of R289 and a credit of R139, there is a balance of R150 (the imprest amount). The R150 is brought down as the opening balance for April.

PETTY CASH BOOK OF BONA ELECTRICAL FOR MARCH 1996

Debit side   Credit side   PCB1

Day	Details	Amount	Day	Details	Vouch	Total	Post	Stat	Sund
1	Bal	150	4	Stamps	1	15	15		
31	Bank	139	8	Clean	2	23			23
			11	Stat	3	11		11	
			15	Wages	4	45			45
			17	Stat	5	27		27	
			24	Donat	6	10			10
			27	Post	7	8	8		
						139	23	38	78
				Bal c/d		150			
		289				289			
Apr									
1	Bal b/d								

Posting from the petty cash book

The petty cash book is the ledger account for petty cash just as the cash book is the ledger account for bank. Therefore all the entries in the petty cash book are already in the petty cash ledger account. However, we must still post the other half of each transaction to the appropriate ledger account.

It was previously said that when a cheque is cashed to replenish the petty cash, the petty cash book is debited and the cash book is credited. Therefore, there is no need to post from the debit side of the petty cash book.

However, all the entries on the credit side of the petty cash book must be posted:

1. The analysis columns TOTALS are posted to appropriate ledger accounts. In our example, R23 must be posted to the debit side of the postage account while R38 must be posted to the debit side of the stationery account.
2. Then the entries in the sundries column are posted **separately** to the appropriate ledger accounts.

Ledger

POSTAGE ACCOUNT — 36

1996			
Mar 31	Petty cash	PCB1	23

STATIONERY ACCOUNT — 37

1996			
Mar 31	Petty cash	PCB1	38

CLEANING MATERIALS — 38

1996			
Mar 8	Petty cash	PCB1	23

WAGES ACCOUNT — 39

1996			
Mar 15	Petty cash	PCB1	45

DONATIONS ACCOUNT — 40

1996			
Mar 24	Petty cash	PCB1	10

Once the petty cash book has been posted, there are equal debits and credits. The folio references are shown in the petty cash book as follows:

PETTY CASH BOOK OF BONA ELECTRICAL FOR MARCH 1996

Debit side   Credit side   PCB1

Day	Details	Amount	Day	Details	Vouch	Total	Post	Stat	Sun
1	Bal	150	4	Stamps	1	15	15		
31	Bank	139	8	Clean	2	23			23 L38
			11	Stat	3	11		11	
			15	Wages	4	45			45 L39
			17	Stat	5	27		27	
			24	Dona	6	10			10 L40
			27	Post	7	8	8		
						139	23	38	78
				Bal c/d		150	L36	L37	
Apr		289				289			
1	Bal b/d	150							

52

Exercise 8.1

The bookkeeper of Powell and Son kept a petty cash float of R250 on the imprest system. You are required to record the following transactions in the petty cash book which must have the following columns: Wages, Stationery, General office expenses, Sundries. Post to the relevant ledger accounts.

1996

May

1   Balance brought forward, R180,40
     Received a cheque for R69,60
3   Bought milk for R2,80
     Paid for postage stamps R9.00
4   Bought envelopes, R12,10
     Gave a donation to the SPCA, R10,00
7   Paid three casual labourers R15 each
     Bought tea, coffee and sugar, R14,50
10   Received a cheque to restore the float of R250
12   Paid a loan to an employee, R50
15   Bought receipt books, R10,10
20   Bought magazines for reception, R8,80
22   Paid petrol for delivery motor cycle, R15
29   Bought milk for R2,80
31   Received a cheque to restore the float

Exercise 8.2

Presidential Dry Cleaners (owner G. Bush) keeps a columnar petty cash book on a R1 000 float imprest system. Record the following transactions and balance off the petty cash book. Then post to the relevant ledger accounts:

June

1   Cash on hand, R1 000.
2   Bought receipt books, R35.
3   Paid A. Lincoln for plumbing done at G. Bush's house, R120.
5   Refunded R. Reagan for account overpaid, R40.
7   Bought stamps, R100.
8   Bought cakes for G. Washington (an employee's birthday), R60.
     Bought cleaning materials, R60.
     Paid for an advertisement in *Daily News*, R175.
10   Paid a donation to R. Nixon Support Group, R100.
12   Received a cheque for expenditure to date.
15   G. Bush took cash for personal use, R290.
18   Bought stationery, R30.
20   G. Bush returned some cash taken on 15 June, R140.
25   Registered letters to the Receiver of Revenue, R5.

Use columns for Postage, Stationery, Drawings, Sundries and a Total column.

Exercise 8.3

Mafuta and Son have a restaurant business and need to conduct much of their purchases through the petty cash which has a float of R1 000.

Using the information below, write up and balance the petty cash for the period indicated. Note that the petty cash book must have analysis columns for the following expenses: Purchases, Wages, Cleaning, Laundry, Sundry. Finally, post to the relevant ledger accounts.

May

1   Cash on hand, R388,20.
    Bought vegetables, R101,50.
    Paid for cooking oil, R20,60.
2   Received a cheque for R611,80.
    Paid waiters wages, R220.
    Paid for printing of menus, R26,85.
    Bought meat, R407.
    Bought flowers for tables, R20,80.
    Paid for cleaning soaps, R10,10.
    Had tablecloths washed, R48,80.
3   Received a cheque to restore the float to R1 000.
    Bought milk, R8,90.
    Bought vegetables, R76.
    Paid wages for cleaners, R20.
    Bought soft drinks, R88,85.
4   Bought sausages, R203,20.
    Gave a donation to Child Welfare, R20.
5   Bought note pads for waiters, R16,50.
    Bought cups and saucers, R188,10.
6   Bought coffee, sugar and tea, R59,95.
    Paid for serviettes to be washed, R25.
    Bought polish for floor, R56,60.
7   Owner drew for personal use R50.
8   Received a cheque to restore the cash on hand to R1 000.
    Bought meat, R396,60.
    Bought fruit and vegetables, R44,25.
9   Repaired tables, R60.
    Bought liquor, R303.
    Bought postage stamps, R8.
    Paid wages, R110.

Exercise 8.4

Your petty cash book is kept on an imprest system with the following analyses columns: Postage, Stationery, Telephone, Wages, Transport, Sundries.

Put through the following transactions and post to the appropriate ledger accounts:

54

1996
April
1   Balance brought forward, R1 000.
2   Paid for franking machine stamps, R204,73.
5   Bought envelope, R86,55.
7   Paid March telephone account, R247,82.
12   Bulk postage on marketing survey, R190,91.
13   Railage on a parcel, R180,55.
14   Bought pencils, R28,91.
16   Drew a cheque for expenditure to date.
17   Cartage, R179,27.
20   Repairs to broken window, R133,27.
22   Stamps, R27,27.
27   Tea and sugar, R22,91.
28   Cleaning materials, R90,90.
30   Casual wages, R345.
30   Postage, R58,18.

At month end, restore the petty cash to the imprest amount.

Exercise 8.5

SMALL BOX MAKERS operate a petty cash book with an imprest amount of R150. Using a columnar format with provision for Postage, Stationery, Office expenses, Wages and Sundries, write up and balance the petty cash book as at 8 May 1996 and post to the relevant ledger accounts:

May

1	Balance brought forward	R78,10
	Received cheque from cashier	R71,90
	Bought stamps	R16
	Paid casual wages	R10
2	Bought milk	R 3,50
	Bought pencils and paper	R 6,20
	Bought floor polish	R 5,90
3	Received a cheque to restore the imprest amount	
4	Paid casual wages	R15
	Gave a donation to the SPCA	R10
	Paid petrol for delivery scooter	R20
5	Bought milk	R 3,50
	Bought light bulbs	R10,20
	Paid for registered post	R 7,50
	Bought envelopes	R15
6	Bought flowers for office reception area	R15
7	Received a cheque to restore the float	
8	Bought sugar	R 4,95
	Paid casual wages	R20
	Bought newspapers and magazines	R11,20

CHAPTER NINE

Sales Journal and Sales Returns Journal

A.   INTRODUCTION

So far, you know that all cash transactions are entered into the cash book. The cash book is really the ledger account for bank. So each cash transaction is entered into the cash book and is posted to one or other ledger account. Also, all petty cash transactions are first entered into the petty cash book and then posted.

B.   THE SALES JOURNAL

But what about transactions in which no cash is involved? For example, if goods are sold on credit, no money changes hands and therefore this transaction does not belong in the cash book.

In Chapter 4, you were shown that a sale on credit is entered directly into the ledger. Remember that you debit the **debtor's account** and credit the **sales account**. But now, there is a new rule:

> No transaction is ever entered directly into the ledger. It first goes through the cash book, the petty cash book or a subsidiary journal.

All **sales of goods on credit** are first entered into the **sales journal** and from there are posted to the ledger.

The sales journal, the cash book and the petty cash book are called **books of first entry**. They are also known as subsidiary books or subsidiary journals.

The reason why transactions are first entered into these books of first entry is to save time on the posting to the ledger. In the previous chapter, you saw how the Sales and Debtors columns can save time in posting one total rather than many separate amounts. In the same way the sales journal, and other subsidiary journals, save time by posting totals rather than each individual amount.

Remember, if goods are sold on credit, this is first entered into the sales journal and is then posted to the ledger. The accounting process now looks as follows:

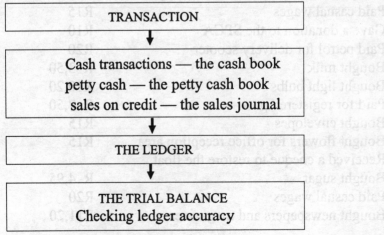

56

Splitting the ledger

In previous exercises, there was only one ledger. From now on, we are going to split the ledger into three separate sections:

1. The debtors' ledger — this contains all debtors' accounts.
2. The creditors' ledger — this contains all creditors accounts.
3. The general ledger — this contains all other accounts.

The folio **DL** will be used for the Debtors' Ledger.
The folio **CL** will be used for the Creditors' Ledger.
The folio **L** will be used for the General Ledger.

Set out of the sales journal

Only goods sold on credit are entered into the sales journal. Remember that goods sold for cash are entered into the cash book.

The sales journal is set out as follows:

SALES JOURNAL OF _____FOR_____1996   SJ1

Inv No	Day	Details (Name of debtor)	Fol	Amount

The page reference

On the top right hand corner, the reference SJ1 appears. It tells us that this is the first page of the sales journal. When information is posted to the ledger, the page reference is shown in the ledger account to indicate where the information was posted from.

The invoice number

When you sell goods on credit, you (the seller) give the original invoice to the buyer. (Remember that you must always think of yourself as the owner of the business). You also keep a copy of the invoice as proof that the transaction took place. The invoice is known as the source document for the sale of goods on credit. Therefore the invoice numbers always appear in the sales journal in strict number order.

Details (name of debtor) and amount

The name of the debtor is entered into the sales journal. This person or company now owes you money. The amount that each debtor owes you is shown in the **Amount** column.

Example 9.1

Enter these transactions into the sales journal of Allicats for March 1996, and then post to the ledger.

1996

March

5 Sold goods on credit to N. Brand for R50 (invoice 9)
9 Clothing articles sold on credit to B. Cool, R90
15 Clothing goods sold to P. Swift, R30 (invoice 11)
24 K. Button bought goods on account for R60

SALES JOURNAL OF ALLICATS FOR MARCH 1996   SJ 1

Inv No	Day	Details (Name of Debtor)	Fol	Amount
9	5	N. Brand		50,00
10	9	B. Cool		90,00
11	15	P. Swift		30,00
12	24	K. Button		60,00
				230,00

Since all the transactions are sales of goods on credit, they are entered into the sales journal. Notice that the invoice numbers run in strict number order.

The Amount column is added up at the end of the month. We now post the entries into the ledger.

Remember that whenever goods are sold on credit, we must put through two entries:

1. The debtors' account is debited (in the debtors' ledger).
2. The sales account is credited (in the general ledger).

Debtors' ledger

N. BRAND — 3

1996				
March 5	Sales	SJ1	50,00	

B. COOL — 4

1996				
March 9	Sales	SJ1	90,00	

P. SWIFT — 5

1996				
March 15	Sales	SJ1	30,00	

K. BUTTON — 6

1996				
March 24	Sales	SJ1	60,00	

Now, we must credit the sales account. But, instead of crediting it with four separate amounts for each sale, we can save time by crediting the sales account with the total credit sales.

58

General ledger

	1996
	Mar 31 Debtors SJ1 230,00

Notice that this entry is only put through at the end of the month once the sales journal has been totalled. Since we cannot list the names of all the debtors, we simply write the word **debtors** in the details column.

This completes the double entry. Assets are increased through a debit to the debtors' accounts. Income is increased by means of a credit to the sales account.

Once the sales journal has been posted, it looks as follows:

SALES JOURNAL OF ALLICATS FOR MARCH 1996   SJ 1

Inv No	Day	Details (name of debtor)	Fol	Amount
9	5	N. Brand	DL3	50,00
10	9	B. Cool	DL4	90,00
11	15	P. Swift	DL5	30,00
12	24	K. Button	DL6	60,00
		Credit sales account		230,00

L23

Take special note that the sales journal is not a ledger account. Therefore we must post both debits and credits to the ledger. Furthermore, the debits and credits posted to the ledger are always equal in value.

C.   THE SALES RETURNS JOURNAL

If goods bought on credit are returned by the buyer, this is entered into the sales returns journal.

Goods that are defective or unsuitable may be returned by the buyer. If the seller accepts that the goods were justifiably returned, then a credit note is issued to the buyer/debtor reducing his debt by the value of the goods returned.

The accounting process now looks as follows:

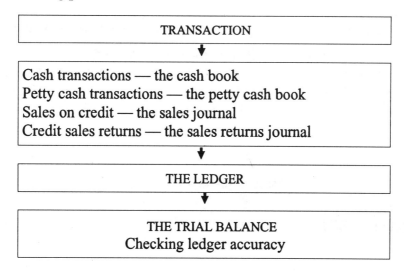

TRANSACTION
↓
Cash transactions — the cash book Petty cash transactions — the petty cash book Sales on credit — the sales journal Credit sales returns — the sales returns journal
↓
THE LEDGER
↓
THE TRIAL BALANCE Checking ledger accuracy

The sales returns journal is set out as follows:

SALES RETURNS JOURNAL OF_____FOR _____1996   SRJ1

Cr Note	Day	Details (name of debtor)	Fol	Amount

The sales returns journal is set out in the same way as the sales journal, except that the source document is a credit note.

Example 9.2

The following transactions are to be recorded in the sales returns journal of Allicats for April 1996. Post this information to the relevant ledger accounts.

1996
April
4   B. Cool returned goods to the value of R10. Issued him with credit note A12.
7   Goods returned by K. Button, R5 (credit note A13).

SALES RETURNS JOURNAL OF ALLICATS FOR APRIL 1996   SRJ1

Cr Note	Day	Details (name of debtor)	Fol	Amount
A12	4	B. Cool		10,00
A13	7	K. Button		5,00
		Debit sales returns		15,00

Since all the transactions are returns of goods sold on credit, they are entered into the sales returns journal. Notice that the credit note numbers run in strict order.

The Amount column is added up at the end of the month. We now post the entries into the ledger.

Whenever goods sold on credit are returned, we put through the following entries:

1.   The sales returns account is debited (in the general ledger).
2.   The debtors' accounts are credited (in the debtors' ledger). Each debtor listed in the sales returns journal is credited with the value of goods returned by him, as he now owes us less, i.e. an asset has decreased. This is done as follows:

General ledger

SALES RETURNS — 24

1996
Apr 30   Debtors   SRJ1   15,00

60

Notice that this entry is only put through at the end of the month once the sales returns journal has been totalled. Since we cannot list the names of all the debtors, we simply write the word **debtors** in the details column.

The sales returns account is debited with the total in the amount column (R15). This debit entry could also be put through directly to the sales account thus reducing the value of our sales. However, it is better to use the sales returns account so that we have a separate record of the value of goods being returned to us. This allows sales returns to be compared to sales to see if the returns are unacceptably high. A very high level of returns may indicate that our goods are inferior.

Debtors' ledger

B. COOL — 4

1996				1996			
Mar 9	Sales	SJ1	90,00	Apr 4	Sales returns	SRJ1	10,00

K. BUTTON — 6

1996				1996			
Mar 24	Sales	SJ1	60,00	Apr 7	Sales returns	SRJ1	5,00

The debtors now owe less since they returned some of the goods sold to them. B. Cool now only owes R80 while K. Button owes R55.

This completes the double entry. Income is decreased by means of a debit to the sales returns account. Assets are also decreased by means of a credit to the debtors's accounts. Do you see that total debits and total credits in the ledger are again equal?

Once the sales returns journal has been posted, it looks as follows:

SALES RETURNS JOURNAL OF ALLICATS FOR APRIL 1996   SRJ1

Cr Note	Day	Details (name of debtor)	Fol	Amount
A12	4	B. Cool	DL4	10,00
A13	7	K. Button	DL6	5,00
		Debit sales returns account		15,00

L24

Exercise 9.1

Enter the appropriate transactions for RAMSEY STORES into the sales journal and sales returns journal. Close off the journals at the end of the month and post to the ledger.

1996
Oct

3   Sold goods on credit to R. Phiri, R560 (invoice 54).
5   Invoiced B. Kopane for goods sold (invoice 55), R240.
7   Sold goods to B. Samsom for cash, R170.
9   R. Phiri returned goods valued at R40 (credit note 5).
14   Sold goods to B. Waters for R230 (invoice 56).

18   Sent credit note 6 to B. Kopane for goods returned, R40.
23   D. Findlay bought goods on credit for R110.
27   Sold goods on credit to R. Phiri for R430 (invoice 58).
29   Goods returned by B. Waters, R25.

Exercise 9.2
Select and enter the appropriate transactions into the sales journal and sales returns journal of Dice Stores. Close off the journals at the end of the month and post to the ledger:

1997
Jan
1   Goods sold on credit to J. Smythe, R150 (invoice 113).
5   Cash sales, R500.
8   Sales on credit to B. Khumalo, R380 and F. Barnes, R610.
15   Paid the telephone account by cheque, R180.
22   J. Smythe returned goods to the value of R20 (credit note 18).
28   H. Louw, a debtor pays R360 on account.
29   F. Barnes returns goods to the value of R35.
30   Sold goods to M. Zulu for R420 (invoice 116).

CHAPTER TEN

Purchases Journal and Purchases Returns Journal

A. THE PURCHASES JOURNAL

So far, we know that all cash transactions are first entered into the cash book. All petty cash transactions are first entered into the petty cash book. All sales of goods on credit are first entered into the sales journal. All returns of goods sold on credit are entered into the sales returns journal.

In this chapter, we introduce two more journals:

1. All purchases of goods on credit are entered in the PURCHASES JOURNAL.
2. All returns of goods purchased on credit are entered in the PURCHASES RETURNS JOURNAL.

The accounting process now looks as follows:

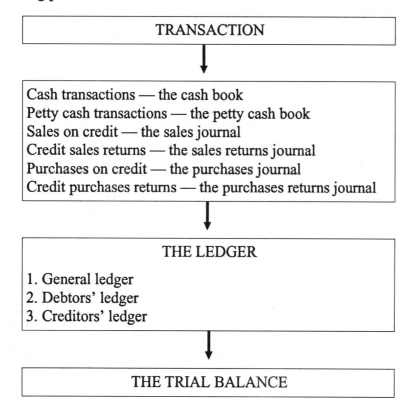

TRANSACTION

Cash transactions — the cash book
Petty cash transactions — the petty cash book
Sales on credit — the sales journal
Credit sales returns — the sales returns journal
Purchases on credit — the purchases journal
Credit purchases returns — the purchases returns journal

THE LEDGER

1. General ledger
2. Debtors' ledger
3. Creditors' ledger

THE TRIAL BALANCE

The purchases journal is set out as follows:

PURCHASES JOURNAL OF_____FOR_____1996   **PJ1**

Inv No	Day	Details (name of creditor)	Fol	Amount

The page reference
On the top right hand corner, the reference PJ1 appears. It tells us that this is the first page of the purchases journal. When entries are posted to the ledger, the page reference is shown in the ledger account to indicate where the information was posted from.

The invoice number
When goods are bought on credit, you receive an original invoice from the seller. (Remember that you must always think of yourself as the owner of the business.) Since the invoices are received from a variety of sellers, they will not be in any kind of order.

Details (name of creditor) and amount
The name of the creditor is entered into the purchases journal. You now owe money to this person or business. The amount that you owe to each creditor is shown in the Amount column.

Example 10.1
Enter the following transactions into the purchases journal of Allicats for March 1996. At month end, post the information into the relevant ledger accounts.

1996
March
11   Bought goods on credit from Jaybee Supplies, R1 500 (invoice 358).
26   Purchased dresses and shirts from Dreshirt (Pty) Ltd for R1 000 (invoice 90B).

PURCHASES JOURNAL OF ALLICATS FOR MARCH 1996   **PJ 1**

Inv No	Day	Details (name of creditor)	Fol	Amount
358	11	Jaybee Supplies	CL3	1 500,00
90B	26	Dreshirt (Pty) Ltd	CL4	1 000,00
		Debit purchases account		2 500,00

L20

Whenever goods are bought on credit, the following entries are put through:

1.   The purchases account is debited (in the general ledger), since an expense is increased.
2.   Creditors' accounts are credited (in the creditors' ledger) as liabilities are increased.

This is done as follows:

General ledger

PURCHASES ACCOUNT — 20

1996			
March 31	Creditors	PJ1	2 500

Notice that this entry is dated for the end of the month once the purchases journal has been closed off. The purchases account is debited with the total of the purchases journal. The page reference from the purchases journal (PJ1) is shown in the folio column. Instead of listing the names of the creditors from whom goods were bought, the word **creditors** is shown in the details column.

The creditors' accounts appear as follows:

Creditors' ledger

JAYBEE SUPPLIES — 3

	1996			
	March 11	Purchases	PJ1	1 500,00

DRESHIRT (PTY) LTD — 4

	1996			
	March 26	Purchases	PJ1	1 000,00

B.   THE PURCHASES RETURNS JOURNAL

When goods bought on credit are returned to suppliers, an entry is recorded in the purchases returns journal.

The purchases returns journal is set out as follows:

PURCHASES RETURNS JOURNAL OF _____ FOR _____1996   PRJ1

Dr Note	Day	Details (name of creditor)	Fol	Amount

Note that the debit note is used when purchases are returned to the supplier. It is sent to the supplier/creditor along with the goods that are being returned. It serves to inform the supplier that their account is to be debited.

Example 10.2

Enter the following transactions into the purchases returns journal of Allicats for April 1996.

1996
April
3   Returned defective goods to Dreshirt (Pty) Ltd along with debit note 501 for R150.
9   Damaged goods sent back to Jaybee Supplies, R75 (debit note 502).

PURCHASES RETURNS JOURNAL OF ALLICATS FOR APRIL 1996   PRJ1

Dr Note	Day	Details (name of creditor)	Fol	Amount
501	3	Dreshirt (Pty) Ltd		150,00
502	9	Jaybee Supplies		75,00
		Credit purchases returns account		225,00

Since all the transactions are returns of credit purchases, they are entered into the purchases returns journal.

The Amount column is added up at the end of the month. We now post the entries into the ledger.

Whenever goods bought on credit are returned to the supplier, the following entries are put through:

1.   The creditors' accounts are debited (in the creditors' ledger).
2.   The purchases returns account is credited (in the general ledger).

General ledger

PURCHASES RETURNS ACCOUNT — 33

		1996			
		April 30	Creditors	PRJ1	225,00

The individual creditors' accounts are debited with the amounts returned to each creditor. Put through these postings yourself.

Creditors' ledger

JAYBEE SUPPLIES — 3

		1996			
		March 11	Purchases	PJ1	1 500,00

DRESHIRT (PTY) LTD — 4

		1996			
		March 26	Purchases	PJ1	1 000,00

Do you see that we now owe Jaybee Supplies R1 425,00 and we owe Dreshirt (Pty) Ltd R850,00?

66

Once the posting have been put through, the purchases returns journal looks as follows:

PURCHASES RETURNS JOURNAL OF ALLICATS FOR APRIL 1996   PRJ1

Dr Note	Day	Details (name of creditor)	Fol	Amount
501	3	Dreshirt (Pty) Ltd	CL4	150,00
502	9	Jaybee Supplies	CL3	75,00
		Credit purchases returns account		225,00

L33

Exercise 10.1

Enter the following transactions into the correct subsidiary journals of Comfy Furniture, a retail furniture outlet. Close off the journals on 30 September, and post to the relevant ledger accounts.

1996

Sept

2   Bought stocks of furniture from Woody Tables for R2 700 (invoice 45).

5   Purchased merchandise on credit for R4 500. Received invoice number 785A from Ron Carvar & Sons.

9   Sale of goods on credit to D. Baxter, R260 (invoice 1).

12   Returned a spoilt table to Woody Tables along with debit note 30 for R150.

14   M. Min bought a dining room table on credit for R310.

19   D. Baxter sent back a chair with a torn cushion, R50. He was sent credit note C1.

22   Sold goods on credit to The Eagle Sports Club, R2 700.

23   Debit note and damaged goods returned to Ron Carvar & Sons, R300.

27   Bought office desks from Office Manufacturing, R5 300 (invoice 4367).

29   Goods damaged in transit returned by The Eagle Sports Club, R400.

Exercise 10.2

Prepare the purchases, sales, purchases returns and sales returns journals to record the following transactions in the books of Cane and Able. All transactions are on credit.

Mar

1   Bought goods from OK Traders — R760,20

2   B. Brown bought goods for R99,80; Sold merchandise to B. Bat for R106,20; B. Blue sold goods to Cane and Able for R64,70; Gave KO Stores a credit note for R16,60.

3   Purchased from KO Stores goods to the value of R94; Received credit note from B. Blue, R10,80; Sold goods to Round Two for R88,50; KO Stores purchased goods worth R64,20.

4   Returned for credit R70 goods bought from OK Traders; Sold goods to Batter & Co, R1703; Purchased from OK Traders, R550; Sold goods to Blood and Sons, R474,40.

5	Issued credit note to Round One for goods returned R6,40; Bought goods from Round One, R101,20; Received a credit note from Balter & Co for goods returned R106; Sold merchandise to KO Stores, R840.
6	Bought merchandise for resale from OK Traders for R520,20; Received a credit note for R10,10 from Round One; Sold goods to OK Traders, R48,50; Sold goods to Cornerman & Co, R147; OK Traders purchased goods worth R63; Issued a credit to KO Stores for their purchases on 5 March.
7	Received a credit from OK Traders, R26,20; Sold goods to Ref Ltd, R69,50; Bought from Bargen and Sons, R190; Purchased from Slam Bazaars, R58,60; Sold goods to Pink Eye Shop for R96,40; Issued a credit to Cornerman & Co for R10 as an allowance for an overcharge.

Exercise 10.3

Write up the following transactions in the appropriate subsidiary books of C. Cherry. All transactions are on credit.

March

1	Sold goods on credit to B. Baya, R101.
2	Purchased stock on credit from A. Customa, R230.
3	B. Baya returns some of his previous purchases, R26.
4	Bought goods on credit from D. Deala, R301.
5	D. Delta purchased goods, R260.
6	Purchases from M. Maka, R490.
7	D. Deala sends a credit note for goods returned to him, R86.
8	Sold goods on credit to B. Baya, R808.
9	C. Customa purchases goods on credit, R585.
10	Sold goods on credit to S. Supplya, R88.
11	Buy goods for resale from AB Wholesalers, R760.
12	Received a credit note for a 10% discount on purchases from AB Wholesalers.
13	Sold goods on credit to N. Neva for R960.
14	The invoice sent to N. Neva on 14 March was incorrectly added up and should have been R1 060. This needs to be corrected.
15	C. Church buys goods worth R85.
16	Sold goods on credit to D. Delta, R462.
17	Bought goods for resale from R. Retaila, R68.
18	Purchased stock on credit from S. Supplya, R495.
19	D. Deala purchased stock on credit, R260.
20	Sent a credit note to D. Deala for items returned, R58.
21	Received a credit note from R. Retaila for returning the goods purchased from him on 18 March.
22	Sold goods on credit to B. Baya, R650.

CHAPTER ELEVEN

Control Accounts

A.   INTRODUCTION

In Chapter 9, the ledger was divided into three sections. Can you remember what they are? Write down your answer in the block below:

```




```

Did you remember that they were the debtors' ledger, the creditors' ledger and the general ledger?

All debtors' accounts are kept in the debtors' ledger and all creditors' accounts are kept in the creditors' ledger. All other accounts are kept in the general ledger.

Let's suppose that you are the bookkeeper for ABC Ltd. Your supervisor asks you how much money is owed in total by the debtors of ABC Ltd. You would have to go to the debtors' ledger and add up each debtor's balance until you arrived at a total. If you are asked how much ABC Ltd owes to its creditors, you would have to add up all the balances in the creditors' ledger. It would waste a lot of time doing this.

However, there is an easier way of knowing how much is owed in total by debtors and how much is owed in total to creditors. We can make use of control accounts.

B.   THE DEBTORS' CONTROL ACCOUNT

In order to keep control of how much is owed by our debtors in total, we open up a control account in the **general ledger**. This account is a summary of all the entries contained in the debtor's ledger. There is only one rule that you must observe when writing up a debtors' control account:

> Whatever you do to a debtor's account, you must do the same to the debtors' control account.

Let's look at how each subsidiary book can be adapted to cope with the debtor's control account:

1. The sales journal

Remember that all sales on credit are entered into the sales journal. From Chapter 9, you may recall that our example of a sales journal was as follows:

SALES JOURNAL OF ALLICATS FOR MARCH 1996 | | | | | SJ 1

Inv No	Day	Details (name of debtor)	Fol	Amount
9	5	N. Brand	DL3	50,00
10	9	B. Cool	DL4	90,00
11	15	P. Swift	DL5	30,00
12	24	K. Button	DL6	60,00
		Credit sales account		230,00

L23

Each credit sale is posted to the debit side of each debtor's account in the debtors' ledger. Remember our rule states **whatever you do to a debtor's account, you must do the same to the control**. Therefore, we will also post (the total) to the debit side of the debtors' control account in the general ledger.

The debtors' ledger contains four accounts (Brand, Cool, Swift and Button) each with a debit entry for the amount of each sale. In the debtors' control account, there will be one debit amount of R230. Therefore, what is contained in the debtors' ledger separately is also contained in the debtors' control account in one amount.

The debtors' control account now looks as follows:

DEBTORS' CONTROL ACCOUNT

1996			
Mar 31	Sales	SJ1	230

2. The sales returns journal

Remember that all returns of goods sold on credit are entered into the sales returns journal. From Chapter 9, the sales returns journal appears as follows:

SALES RETURNS JOURNAL OF ALLICATS FOR APRIL 1996 | | | | | SRJ1

Cr Note	Day	Detail (name of debtor)	Fol	Amount
A12	4	B. Cool	DL4	10,00
A13	7	K. Button	DL6	5,00
		Debit sales returns account		15,00

L24

Since the debtors' accounts are credited in the debtors' ledger, so must the debtors control account be credited with the total (R15). The posting to the debtors' control account is entered as follows:

DEBTORS CONTROL ACCOUNT

1996				1996			
Mar 31	Sales	SJ1	230,00	Apr 30	Sales returns	SRJ1	15,00

The balance on the debtors' control account is now R215. This amount is the same as the sum of balances on the individual debtors' accounts in the debtors' ledger. (Brand R50 + Cool R80 + Swift R30 + Button R55 = R215). These debtors' accounts are shown below:

Debtors' ledger

N. BRAND — 3

1996				
March 5	Sales	SJ1	50,00	

B.COOL — 4

1996				1996			
March 9	Sales	SJ1	90,00	Apr 4	Sales returns	SRJ1	10,00

P. SWIFT — 5

1996				
March 15	Sales	SJ1	30,00	

K. BUTTON — 6

1996				1996			
March 24	Sales	SJ1	60,00	Apr 7	Sales returns	SRJ1	5,00

3. The cash book (cash receipts section)

When the debtors pay their debts, an entry is made in the cash receipts section of the cash book. Assume that B. Cool pays R60,00 and P. Button pays R30,00.

CASH RECEIPTS FOR APRIL 1996　　　　　　　　　　　　　　　　　　　　　CB 1

Doc	Date	Details	Folio	Sundries	Sales	Debtors	Bank
BDS	2	CAPITAL		1 000			1 000
CSS	5	SALES			150		150
REC	8	B. Cool				60	60
CSS	19	SALES			240		240
REC	29	P. Button				30	30
				1 000	390	90	

From the cash receipts book, the debtors' accounts in the debtors' ledger are credited. Therefore, the debtors' control account must also be credited with the total of debtors' payments. In the above Cash Receipts section, Cool is credited with R60 while Button is credited with R30. Therefore we must credit the debtors' control account with the total of the debtors' column (R90). The debtors' control now appears as follows:

DEBTORS' CONTROL ACCOUNT

1996				1996			
Mar 31	Sales	SJ1	230,00	Apr 30	Sales Returns	SRJ1	15,00
					Bank	CB1	90,00

The balance on the debtors' control account is now R125. This is equal to the total of the debtors' accounts in the debtors' ledger. (Brand R50 + Cool R20 + Swift R30 + Button R25 = R125). Cool and Button's accounts appear below:

Debtors' ledger

B. COOL — 4

1996					1996				
March 9	Sales	SJ1		90,00	Apr 4	Sales returns	SRJ1		10,00
					8	Bank	CB1		60,00

K. BUTTON — 6

1996					1996				
March 24	Sales	SJ1		60,00	Apr 4	Sales returns	SRJ1		5,00
					29	Bank	CB1		30,00

At all times, the balance on the debtors' control account is equal to the total of the debtors' balances in the debtors' ledger. Therefore, when you draw up a trial balance, you need only include the balance on the debtors' control account. It is the balance on the debtors' control account that shows how much debtors owe us in total.

C. THE CREDITORS' CONTROL ACCOUNT

In order to determine how much we owe our creditors, we open up a creditors' control account in the **general ledger**. This account is a summary of all entries contained in the creditors' ledger. There is only one rule that you must observe when writing up a creditors' control account:

> Whatever you do to a creditor's account, you must do the same to the creditors' control account.

Let's look at how each subsidiary book can be adapted to cope with the creditors' control account:

1. The purchases journal

Remember that all purchases on credit are entered into the purchases journal. From Chapter 10, you may recall that our example of a purchases journal was as follows:

PURCHASES JOURNAL OF ALLICATS FOR MARCH 1996   PJ 1

Inv No	Day	Details (name of creditor)	Fol	Amount
358	11	Jaybee Supplies		1 500,00
90B	26	Dreshirt (Pty) Ltd		1 000,00
		Debit purchases account		2 500,00

Each credit purchase is posted to the credit side of each creditor's account in the creditors' ledger. Remember our rule states **whatever you do to a creditor's account,**

you must do the same to the control. Therefore, we also post the total of R2 500 to the credit side of the creditors' control account in the general ledger.

This means that the creditors' ledger will contain two accounts each with a credit entry for the amount of the purchase. Jaybee's account is credited with R1 500 while Dreshirt's account is credited with R1 000. In the creditors' control account, there is one credit amount of R2 500. Therefore, what is contained in the creditors' ledger separately is also contained in the creditors' control account in one amount.

The creditors' control account now looks as follows:

CREDITORS' CONTROL ACCOUNT

	1996			
	Mar 31	Purchases	PJ1	2 500

2. The purchase returns journal

Remember that all returns of goods bought on credit are entered into the purchases returns journal. From Chapter 10, the purchases returns journal appears as follows:

PURCHASES RETURNS JOURNAL OF ALLICATS FOR APRIL 1996   PRJ1

Dr Note	Day	Details (name of creditor)	Fol	Amount
501	3	Dreshirt (Pty) Ltd		150,00
502	9	Jaybee Supplies		75,00
		Credit purchases returns account		225,00

Since the creditors' accounts are debited in the creditors' journal, so must the creditors control account be debited with the total (R225). The creditors' control account now appears as follows:

CREDITORS' CONTROL ACCOUNT

1996				1996			
Apr 30	Purch returns	PRJ1	225	Mar 31	Purchases	PJ1	2 500

The balance on the creditors' control account is now R2 275. This amount is the same as the sum of balances on the individual creditors' accounts in the creditors' ledger. (Jaybee R1 425 + Dreshirt R850 = R2 275). These accounts appear below:

Creditors' ledger

JAYBEE SUPPLIES — 3

1996				1996			
Apr 9	Purch returns	PRJ1	75	Mar 11	Purchases	PJ1	1 500

DRESHIRT (PTY) LTD — 4

1996				1996			
Apr 3	Purch returns	PRJ1	150	Mar 26	Purchases	PJ1	1 000

3. The cash payments section of the cash book

When we pay our creditors, an entry is made in the Cash Payments section of the cash book. Assume that we pay Jaybee R425,00 and we pay Dreshirt R500,00.

CASH PAYMENTS APRIL 1996   CB 1

Cheq	Date	Details	Fol	Sundries	Purch	Creditors	Bank
001	4	Advertising	L11	120			120
002	8	Jaybee	L14			425	425
003	13	Purchases			890		890
004	14	Telephone	L12	50			50
005	21	Dreshirt	L15			500	500
006	27	Purchases			450		450
B\S	30	Bank Charges	L13	10			10
				180	1 340	925	2 445

From the cash payments, we debit the creditor's accounts in the creditors' ledger. Therefore, the creditors' control account must also be debited with the total of payments to creditors. In the above Cash Payments section, Jaybee is debited with R425 while Dreshirt is debited with R500. Therefore we must debit the creditors' control account with the total of the creditors' column (R925). The creditors' control account now appears as follows:

CREDITORS' CONTROL ACCOUNT

1996				1996			
Mar 31	Purch returns	PRJ1	225,00	Mar 31	Purchases	PJ1	2 500,00
	Bank	CB1	925,00				

The balance on the creditors' control account is now R1 350. This is equal to the total of creditors accounts in the creditors' ledger. (Jaybee R1 000 + Dreshirt R350 = R1 350). These accounts are shown below:

Creditors' ledger

JAYBEE SUPPLIES — 3

1996				1996			
Apr 9	Purch returns	PRJ1	75,00	Mar 11	Purchases	PJ1	1500,00
8	Bank	CB1	425,00				

DRESHIRT (PTY) LTD — 4

1996				1996			
Apr 3	Purch returns	PRJ1	150,00	Mar 26	Purchases	PJ1	1 000,00
21	Bank	CB1	500,00				

At all times, the balance on the creditors' control account is equal to the total of the balances in the creditors' ledger. Therefore, when you draw up a trial balance, you need only include the balance on the creditors' control account. This amount shows how much is owing to creditors in total.

You may be wondering why we need the debtors' and creditors' ledger now that we have control accounts. The answer is that control accounts are only able to show how much is owed in total by debtors or to creditors. We must still have a record of how much is owed by each individual debtor or to each individual creditor. This information can only be obtained from the debtors' and creditors' ledgers.

Example 11.1

Often, your knowledge of control accounts is tested in questions that are set out like the one below. Go through this example and make sure that you understand the solution.

Write up the debtors' and the creditors' control accounts in the ledger of Wakro Stores for the month of July 1996:

Opening debtors' balances   R5 000
Opening creditors' balances   R4 000

Sales on credit R50 000; Purchases on credit R30 000; Cash sales R5 000; Sales returns (Returns inwards) R3 000; Purchases returns (Returns outwards) R2 000; Payment by debtors R18 000; Payment to creditors R15 000; Bad debts R500; Interest charged on overdue debtors' accounts R300.

DEBTORS' CONTROL ACCOUNT

1996				1996			
July 1	Balance b/d		5 000,00	July 31	Sales return	SRJ1	3 000,00
31	Sales	SJ1	50 000,00		Bank	CB1	18 000,00
	Interest	J1	300,00		Bad debts	J1	500,00
					Balance	c/d	33 800,00
			55 300,00				55 300,00
Aug 1	Balance b/d		33 800,00				

Take note of the following:

1. Since the debtors' control is an asset account, it is increased by means of debit entries and decreased by means of credit entries.
2. Entries for which debtors owe more are recorded on the debit side of the debtors' control account. Therefore sales on credit and interest charged on overdue accounts are shown on the debit side of the debtors' control account.
3. Entries for which debtors owe less are recorded on the credit side of the debtors' control account. Therefore, sales returns, cash payments from debtors (bank) and bad debts are shown on the credit side of the debtors' control account.
4. Cash sales are not shown in the debtors' control account since they do not affect debtors.

1996				1996			
July 31	Purch returns	PRJ1	2 000,00	July 1	Balance	b/d	4 000,00
	Bank	CB1	15 000,00	31	Purchases	PJ1	30 000,00
	Balance	c/d	17 000,00				
			34 000,00				34 000,00
				Aug 1	Balance	b/d	17 000,00

Take note of the following:

1. The creditors' control account is a liability account. Therefore, all entries that increase our liability to our creditors must be credited to the creditors' control account. All entries that decrease our liability to our creditors must be debited to the creditors' control account.
2. Since purchases on credit increase our liability to our creditors, it must be shown on the credit side of the control account.
3. Since purchases returns and payments to creditors decrease our liability, they are debited to the control account.

Exercise 11.1

Write up the debtors' control account and the creditors' control account of Ronnie Wholesalers.

April
1   Opening debtors' balances   R26 880
     Opening creditors' balances   R62 010

Credit purchases R46 805; Returns inwards R2 068; Returns outwards R596; Bad debts written off R300; Credit sales R30 411; Payments of accounts made by Ronnie Wholesalers R3 546; Cash received from customers R20 114; Discount received R490; Discount allowed R606; Cash refunds received from creditors R140; Refunds made to customers R260; Interest charged by suppliers on unpaid accounts R166.

D. IMPORTANT REVISION EXERCISE

S. Sam operates a sporting shop from where he sells sporting equipment. On 1 January 1997, the following balances appear in the ledger of Sam's Sports:

Capital	R17 000
Stock	R12 500
Debtors' control	R 2 000
Bank	R 6 700
Furniture	R 2 600
Shop fittings	R 1 200
Loan — XY Bank	R 5 000
Creditors' control	R 3 000

Debtors

T. Watson	R 500
S. Edberg	R 800
K. Lewis	R 700

Creditors

Racquet Supplies	R1 200
Golf Connection	R1 800

You are required to:

1. Enter the following transactions for January 1997 into the correct subsidiary journals of Sam's Sports.
2. Close off the journals and post to the appropriate ledger accounts.
3. Balance and total the ledger accounts, and take out a trial balance on 31 January 1997.

1997
Jan
3   Bought sporting accessories from Sports World for R800 (invoice 31).
4   Cash sales, R430.
6   Bought stationery from Spikes Stationers and paid by cheque, R80 (cheque no 28).
7   Goods sold on credit to K. Lewis, R250 (invoice 10A).
    Received a cheque from T. Watson for R200 (receipt 3).
8   S. Sam paid his personal garage bill by means of a business cheque, R160
9   Received goods and invoice 596 from Golf Connection, R1 400.
12 Sold second-hand golf balls at a reduced price for cash, R80.
    T. Watson bought golf clubs to the value of R470 (invoice 11A).
13 Sold good on credit to G. Gooch, R410.
14 Received business cards printed by Kemp and Sons and paid by cheque, R50.
16 K. Lewis returned damaged goods to the value of R70. Issued credit note 7.
    Cash sales, R840.
17 Placed an advertisement in *The Tribune* and paid R125.
    Received a commission on the sale of locally-made goods, R220.
19 Drew a cheque in part payment of Golf Connection account, R1 000.
20 Returned defective soccer balls to Sports World along with debit note 17, R100.
21 Received invoice J32 and goods from Racquet Supplies, R500.
23 Cash sales, R160.
    Sold goods in account to S. Edberg, R200.
25 T. Watson returned damaged goods, R50.
26 Paid rent by cheque, R560.
27 Paid on account to Racquet Supplies, R700.
    K. Lewis paid the amount owing on his account.
29 Drew cheque in favour of the Crown Park Municipality for electricity and water, R75.
30 Received Edberg's cheque for R500 in part payment of his account.

31   Cash sales, R940.
      Paid salary to the shop assistant, R850.

Once you have completed this exercise, check your answer against the following model solution.

REVISION EXERCISE – MODEL SOLUTION

PURCHASES JOURNAL OF SAM'S SPORTS FOR JANUARY 1997 — PJ1

Inv no	Day	Details (name of creditor)	Fol	Amount
31	3	Sports World	CL3	800
596	9	Golf Connection	CL2	1 400
J32	21	Raquet Supplies	CL1	500
		Dr Purchases a/c / Cr Creditors' control		2 700
				L8 L7

SALES JOURNAL OF SAM'S SPORTS FOR JANUARY 1997 — SJ1

Inv no	Day	Details (name of creditor)	Fol	Amount
10A	7	K Lewis	DL3	250
11A	12	T Watson	DL1	470
12A	13	G Gooch	DL4	410
13A	23	S Edberg	DL2	200
		Cr Sales a/c / Dr Debtors' control		1 330
				L10 L3

SALES RETURNS JOURNAL OF SAM'S SPORTS FOR JANUARY 1997 — SRJ1

Cr note	Day	Details (name of debtor)	Fol	Amount
7	16	K Lewis	DL3	70
8	25	T Watson	DL1	50
		Dr Sales returns / Cr Debtors' control		120
				L11 L3

PURCHASES RETURNS JOURNAL OF SAM'S SPORTS FOR JANUARY 1997 — PRJ1

Dr note	Day	Details (name of creditor)	Fol	Amount
17	20	Sports World	CL3	100
		Cr Purch returns / Dr Creditors' control		100
				L9 L7

78

CASH BOOK OF SAM'S SPORTS FOR JANUARY 1997 – CASH RECEIPTS SECTION   CB1

Doc	Date	Details	Fol	Sundries	Sales	Debtors	Bank
	1	Balance	b/d	6 700			6 700
CSS	4	Sales			430		430
REC	7	T Watson	DL1			200	200
CSS	12	Sales			80		80
CSS	16	Sales			840		840
REC	17	Comm Rec	L12	220			220
CSS	23	Sales			160		160
REC	27	K Lewis	DL3			880	880
REC	30	S Edberg	DL2			500	500
CSS	31	Sales			940		940
				6 920	2 450	1 580	10 950
					L10	L3	

CASH BOOK OF SAM'S SPORTS FOR JANUARY 1997 — CASH PAYMENTS SECTION   CB1

Cheq	Date	Details	Fol	Sundries	Creditors	Bank
28	6	Stationery	L14	80		80
29	8	Drawings	L15	160		160
30	14	Stationery	L14	50		50
31	17	Advertising	L16	125		125
32	19	Golf Connection	CL2		1 000	1 000
33	26	Rent	L17	560		560
34	27	Raquet Supplies	CL1		700	700
35	29	Elec & water	L13	75		75
36	31	Salaries	L18	850		850
				1 900	1 700	3 600
					L7	

General ledger

CAPITAL ACCOUNT — 1

				1997			
				Jan 1	Balance	b/d	17 000

STOCK ACCOUNT — 2

1997				
Jan 1	Balance	b/d	12 500	

DEBTORS CONTROL ACCOUNT — 3

1997				1997			
Jan 1	Balance b/d		2 000	Jan 31	Bank	CB1	1 580
31	Sales	SJ1	1 330		Sales retr	SRJ1	120
					Balance	c/d	1 630
			3 330				3 330
Feb 1	Balance b/d		1 630				

FURNITURE ACCOUNT — 4

1997			
Jan 1	Balance b/d		2 600

SHOP FITTINGS ACCOUNT — 5

1997			
Jan 1	Balance b/d		1 200

LOAN — XY BANK — 6

				1997			
				Jan 1	Balance	b/d	5 000

CREDITORS CONTROL ACCOUNT — 7

1997				1997			
Jan 31	Bank	CB1	1 700	Jan 1	Balance	b/d	3 000
	Purch ret	PRJ1	100	31	Purchases	PJ1	2 700
	Balance	c/d	3 900				
			5 700				5 700
				Feb 1	Balance	b/d	3 900

PURCHASES ACCOUNT — 8

1997			
Jan 31	Creditors	PJ1	2 700

PURCHASES RETURNS ACCOUNT — 9

			1997			
			Jan 31	Creditors	PRJ1	100

SALES ACCOUNT — 10

			1997			
			Jan 31	Debtors	SJ1	1 330
			31	Bank	CB1	2 450
						3 780

SALES RETURN ACCOUNT — 11

1997							
Jan 31	Debtors	SRJ1	120				

COMMISSION RECEIVED — 12

				1997			
				Jan 17	Bank	CB1	220

ELECTRICITY & WATER — 13

1997							
Jan 29	Bank	CB1	75				

STATIONERY ACCOUNT — 14

1997							
Jan 6	Bank	CB1	80				
14	Bank	CB1	50				
			130				

DRAWINGS ACCOUNT — 15

1997							
Jan 8	Bank	CB1	160				

ADVERTISING ACCOUNT — 16

1997							
Jan 17	Bank	CB1	125				

RENT ACCOUNT — 17

1997							
Jan 26	Bank	CB1	560				

SALARIES ACCOUNT — 18

1997							
Jan 31	Bank	CB1	850				

Debtors' ledger

T. WATSON — 1

1997				1997			
Jan 1	Balance b/d		500	Jan 25	Sales ret	SRJ1	50
12	Sales	SJ1	470	7	Bank	CB1	200
				31	Balance	c/d	720
			970				970
Feb 1	Balance b/d		720				

1997					1997			
Jan 1	Balance b/d		800		Jan 30	Bank	CB1	500
23	Sales	SJ1	200		31	Balance	c/d	500
			1 000					1 000
Feb 1	Balance b/d		500					

1997					1997			
Jan 1	Balance b/d		700		Jan 16	Sales ret	SRJ1	70
7	Sales	SJ1	250		27	Bank	CB1	880
			950					950

1997					1997			
Jan 13	Sales	SJ1	410		Jan 31	Balance	c/d	410
			410					410
Feb 1	Balance b/d		410					

Creditors' ledger

1997					1997			
Jan 27	Bank	CB1	700		Jan 1	Balance	b/d	1 200
31	Balance	c/d	1 000		21	Purchases	PJ1	500
			1 700					1 700
					Feb 1	Balance	b/d	1 000

1997					1997			
Jan 19	Bank	CB1	1 000		Jan 1	Balance	b/d	1 800
31	Balance	c/d	2 200		9	Purchases	PJ1	1 400
			3 200					3 200
					Feb 1	Balance	b/d	2 200

1997				1997			
Jan 20	Purch returns	PRJ1	100	Jan 3	Purchases PJ1		800
31	Balance	c/d	700				
			800				800
				Feb 1	Balance	b/d	700

TRIAL BALANCE OF SAM'S SPORTS AT 31 JANUARY 1997

	DEBIT	CREDIT
Capital		17 000
Stock (1 January 1997)	12 500	
Debtors' control	1 630	
Bank***	7 350	
Furniture	2 600	
Shop fittings	1 200	
Loan — XY Bank		5 000
Creditors' control		3 900
Purchases	2 700	
Purchases returns		100
Sales		3 780
Sales returns	120	
Commission received		220
Electricity & water	75	
Stationery	130	
Drawings	160	
Advertising	125	
Rent	560	
Salaries	850	
	30 000	30 000

*** The bank balance is calculated by subtracting the total cash payments (R3 600) from the total cash receipts (R10 950).

CHAPTER TWELVE

The General Journal

A. INTRODUCTION

This chapter deals with yet another subsidiary journal — the general journal. As the name implies, this journal is not used to record any particular type of transaction. In fact, any transaction can be recorded in this journal.

B. TRANSACTIONS WHICH ARE RECORDED IN THE GENERAL JOURNAL

All transactions that do not belong to a particular subsidiary book or journal are entered into the general journal.

For example, Bob's Bikes sells office furniture on credit to Joe Baker for R100. This transaction cannot be entered into the Cash Receipts section of the cash book since it is on credit. It cannot be recorded in the sales journal, since it is not a sale of goods (trading stock).

Since it does not belong in any of the specialist journals, this transaction is entered in the general journal (hereafter called "the journal")

C. THE SET-OUT OF THE JOURNAL

The journal is set out in such a way that any transaction can be entered into it.

JOURNAL OF _____

Date	Details	Folio	Debit	Credit

The following entry is now recorded in the journal:

1997
Jan
25   Bob's Bikes sells old furniture on credit to Joe Baker for R100.

In terms of the double-entry system, this transaction is recorded by means of a debit to Joe Baker's account (increase in debtors) and a credit to the furniture account (decrease in furniture).

The transaction is entered into the journal as follows:

JOURNAL OF BOB'S BIKES   J1

Date	Details	Folio	Debit	Credit
1997 Jan 25	Joe Baker Furniture (Furniture sold on credit)	DL7/L5 L11	100,00	100,00

Note that:

1. The name of the account to be debited is always written first and on top. The amount is written in the Debit column.
2. The name of the account to be credited is written underneath, and is indented against the margin. The amount is written in the Credit column.
3. Every journal entry is accompanied by a journal narration (written below in brackets). This describes in words what has taken place. The journal narration is necessary since so many different types of transactions are entered into the journal.

D.   POSTING FROM THE JOURNAL TO THE LEDGER

In posting to the ledger, you must carry out the journal instruction. For the given example, we debit Joe Baker's account and credit the furniture account in the ledger. This appear as follows:

Debtors' ledger

JOE BAKER — 7

1997 Jan 25	Furniture	J1	100,00

Joe Baker's account is debited in the debtors' ledger. As always, the name of the other account ("furniture") is written into the details column. The entry is posted from the journal, page 1, and this is shown by means of the folio reference "J1".

The folio reference in the journal reflects that the entry was posted to DL7 (debtors' ledger account 7).

Recall that an entry in the debtors' ledger must be duplicated in the debtors' control account in the general ledger. Therefore, a debit must also be posted to the debit side of the debtors' control account in the general ledger.

General ledger

DEBTORS' CONTROL — 5

1997 Jan 25	Furniture	J1	100,00

The credit is posted to the furniture account in the general ledger as follows:

FURNITURE — 11

	1997			
	Jan 25	Joe Baker	J1	100,00

E. SOME TRANSACTIONS THAT MAY BE ENTERED INTO THE JOURNAL

1. Bad debts

If a debtor is declared insolvent, or is unable to pay part or all of his debt, his account must be written off as a bad debt. This is also known as an **irrecoverable debt**.

The bad debt is an expense and therefore the Bad Debts account is always debited. The account of the debtor is credited since he no longer owes money. (The asset is reduced.)

Put through the following entry yourself and post to the relevant ledger accounts.

On 18 March, 1996, the account of P. Hardup, a debtor owing R50, must be written off as irrecoverable. The entry must be put through the journal of Bob's Bikes.

JOURNAL OF BOB'S BIKES

Date	Details	Folio	Debit	Credit

Now post to the ledger accounts below:

Debtors' ledger

MR HARDUP — 9

1996			
Mar 1	Balance b/d	50,00	

General ledger

BAD DEBTS — 14

DEBTORS' CONTROL — 18

2. Recovering a bad debt written off (not entered into the journal)

Sometimes after a bad debt is written off, the money is received from the defaulting debtor. Mr Hardup's debt of R50 was written off in the previous example. If he pays the debt after it has been written off, this is known as a **bad debt recovered**.

Since the bad debt recovered brings money into the business, this transaction is entered into the cash receipts section of the cash book. This means that the bank account is debited and the bad debts recovered account in the general ledger is credited.

Note that Mr Hardup's account is not affected since his account is already closed off. Enter the receipt of R50 from Mr Hardup as a bad debt recovered in the Cash Receipts section of the cash book below. Then post to the appropriate ledger account.

CASH RECEIPTS   CB1

Doc	Date	Details	Folio	Sundries	Sales	Debtors	Bank

BAD DEBTS RECOVERED — 23

3. Provision for bad debts

We have already seen that some debtors' accounts are written off as bad debts. However, there are other debtors that are unlikely to pay their debts. Instead of waiting for these debts to turn bad, we must estimate what percentage we expect are likely to be bad debts. This is known as creating a provision for bad debts.

Assume that the outstanding debtors in Bob's Bikes total R2 000. It is estimated that 5% of these debtors are unlikely to pay their accounts. Five per cent of R2 000 is R100. Therefore, we must create a provision for bad debts of R100.

In order to create a provision for bad debts of R100, the following entry must be put through:

JOURNAL OF BOB'S BIKES

Date	Details	Folio	Debit	Credit
	Bad debts Provision for bad debts (Creating a provision for bad debts of 5% of outstanding debtors)		100,00	100,00

4. Drawings of Goods

We have already dealt with the owner drawing cash from the business. Recall that this transaction is entered in the Cash Payments section of the cash book (debit drawings and credit bank).

However, if the owner draws goods from the business, this entry is entered into the journal. Since no money changes hands, it cannot be entered into the cash book.

Consider the following example for Bob's Bicycle Shop. If Bob takes home a bicycle to give to his son as a birthday present, then Bob has drawn goods from the business. The drawings account must be debited since drawings is an expense. The Purchases account is credited to show that a bicycle has been taken out of the business.

Enter this transaction into the Journal on 8 August 1996 and post to the ledger:

JOURNAL OF BOB'S BIKES

Date	Details	Folio	Debit	Credit

General ledger

5. Purchase of a fixed asset on credit

The purchase of a fixed asset on credit is also entered into the journal. If Bob's Bikes purchases a vehicle on credit from Sipho's Motors on 1 January 1997 for R5 000, then the following entry is put through:

JOURNAL OF BOB'S BIKES

Date	Details	Folio	Debit	Credit
1997 Jan 1	Vehicles		5 000,00	
	Sipho's Motors			5 000,00
	(Purchase of vehicle on credit)			

6. Correction of errors

The journal is used to correct any mistakes made in writing up the records of the business.

For example, assume that an amount of R50 for petrol was debited by mistake to the Vehicles account.

VEHICLES

1996			
June 6	Bank	CPJ1	50,00

88

This error can be corrected by means of a journal entry, as follows:

JOURNAL OF BOB'S BIKES

Date	Details	Folio	Debit	Credit
1996 Jun 30	Petrol Vehicles (Correction of amount incorrectly debited to vehicles account)		50,00	50,00

The Vehicles account is credited to remove the incorrect debit entry. The R50 is debited to the petrol account where it belongs. Put through the journal entry to the ledger accounts below to see how the error is corrected.

VEHICLES

1996			
June 6	Bank	CPJ1	50,00

PETROL

7. Adjusting journal entries

At the end of an accounting period, there are usually some adjustments that should be put through. Some examples of adjustments that apply to most businesses are as follows:

(a) *Accrued expenses*

Most expenses are paid during the financial year during which they are incurred. Sometimes, an expense incurred towards the end of a financial year may only be paid in the following financial year. This is called an accrued expense since it is still owing at the end of the current financial year.

Example 12.1

Bob's Bikes pays a monthly amount of R100 for electricity and water. At the end of the financial year, 31 December 1996, Bob has still not paid electricity and water for December. Electricity and water has only been paid for 11 months so the account shows a total of R1 100 (11 months × R100 per month).

The journal entry to adjust the electricity and water account is as follows:

JOURNAL OF BOB'S BIKES

Date	Details	Folio	Debit	Credit
1996 Dec 31	Electricity & water Accrued expenses (Electricity & water accrued)	L17	100,00	100,00

The debit to the electricity and water account will increase the amount in this account to R1 200. This is the total cost of electricity and water for 1996.

The electricity and water account now appears as follows:

ELECTRICITY AND WATER — 17

1996			
Dec 31	Total	b/d	1100,00
	Accrued Exp	J1	100,00
			1200,00

The credit to the accrued expenses account appears as follows:

ACCRUED EXPENSES — 21

	1996			
	Dec 31	Water & Elec	J1	100,00

The accrued expenses account is classified as a current liability. This is because Bob's Bikes owes R100 for electricity and water as at 31 December 1996.

(b)   *Prepaid expenses*

Sometimes, an expense is paid in advance. The expense belongs in the next financial period but is paid (in advance) in the current period.

Example 12.2

Bob's Bikes takes out an insurance policy on 28 February 1996. The premium is R100 per month and Bob agrees to pay for a full year in advance. This payment is entered into the Cash Payments section of the cash book and an amount of R1 200 is posted to the debit side of the insurance account.

At the end of Bob's Bikes' financial year, 31 December 1996, insurance is prepaid for January and February 1997. An amount of R1 200 is shown in the insurance account, but R200 of this is in respect of the following financial year. We must put through an adjusting entry so that the correct amount of insurance is accounted for.

The entry is as follows:

JOURNAL OF BOB'S BIKES

1996	Prepaid expenses	L39	200,00	
Dec 31	Insurance	L34		200,00
	(Insurance prepaid)			

In crediting the insurance account with R200, the account is adjusted to show a balance of R1 000 which is payment for 10 months at R100 per month.

The insurance account now appears as follows:

General ledger

<table>
<tr><td colspan="7" align="center">INSURANCE — 34</td></tr>
<tr><td>1996</td><td></td><td></td><td></td><td>1996</td><td></td><td></td></tr>
<tr><td>Feb 28</td><td>Bank</td><td>CPJ3</td><td>1 200,00</td><td>Dec 31</td><td>Prepaid exp   J1</td><td>200,00</td></tr>
</table>

The balance on the insurance account is R1 000. This is the difference between the debit and credit sides in the account above. Remember that this is the cost of insurance that was incurred during 1996.

The prepaid expenses account is debited in the general ledger. This account is classified as a current asset since, at 31 December, we have paid R200 for a future time. Theoretically, we could demand this money back if we decide to cancel the insurance policy.

Since prepaid expenses is a current asset, it has a debit balance. The account appears below:

General ledger

<table>
<tr><td colspan="4" align="center">PREPAID EXPENSES — 39</td></tr>
<tr><td>1996</td><td></td><td></td><td></td></tr>
<tr><td>Dec 31</td><td>Insurance</td><td>J1</td><td>200,00</td></tr>
</table>

(c) *Income received in advance*

Sometimes, income that is owing to a business is received in advance. For example, money owing in respect of January 1997 may be received in December 1996. This is known as income received in advance.

Example 12.3

Commission for January 1997 of R500 is received by Bob's Bikes on 27 December 1996. This entry is recorded into the Cash Receipts section of the cash book and is posted to the credit side of the Commission Received account. At 31 December, put through an adjusting journal entry to show the commission received as income received in advance in the solution box supplied.

JOURNAL OF BOB'S BIKES

Date	Details	Folio	Debit	Credit
	(Commission received in advance)			

Check your answer against the solution that follows:

JOURNAL OF BOB'S BIKES

Date	Details	Folio	Debit	Credit
1996 Dec 31	Commission received Income received in advance (Commission received in advance)		R500,00	R500,00

Now post this journal entry to the relevant accounts below:

COMMISSION RECEIVED — 44

	1996		
	Dec 27	Bank	CB4	500,00

Notice that the commission received in December already appears on the credit side of this account. You should have put through a debit entry to this account which cancels out the credit amount.

INCOME RECEIVED IN ADVANCE — 42

You should have put through a credit entry to this account. Income received in advance is a current liability since Bob's Bikes is holding money that should only have been received in the next financial year. At 31 December, Bob owes this money to the person who paid it to him.

(d)   *Accrued income*
Income may be owing to a company at the end of a financial period. Since this income belongs to the current financial period, it must be brought into this period. This is called accrued income.

Example 12.4
On 31 December 1996, Bob's Bikes has not yet received the rent for December of R750. This is called accrued income.

   Put through the adjusting entry to bring this rent into account for year ended 1996.

JOURNAL OF BOB'S BIKES

Date	Details	Folio	Debit	Credit
	(Rent receivable accrued)			

Now check your entry against the following solution:

JOURNAL OF BOB'S BIKES

Date	Details	Folio	Debit	Credit
1996 Dec 31	Income accrued Rent received (Rent receivable accrued)		750,00	750,00

Income accrued is a current asset and therefore it appears as a debit entry. Rent received is increased by R750 in respect of December's rent.

Now post this entry to the ledger accounts below:

INCOME ACCRUED — 46

You should have debited this current asset account.

RENT RECEIVED — 29

The rent received account is an income account and you should have credited it.

(e)   *Depreciation*

All businesses are likely to have fixed assets of one kind or another. Office furniture, office equipment, vehicles, land and buildings are all examples of fixed assets that a business owns.

However, fixed assets wear out over time. They are worth less and less as they become older. For example, a table costing R300 may only be worth R60 after four years. We say that its value has depreciated over time.

When this table was first purchased, the **office furniture** account was debited with R300. At the end of each financial year, the value of the asset must be depreciated to show how the asset has dropped in value. This is done by means of an adjusting journal entry.

Straight line depreciation

In this method of depreciation, a fixed percentage is written off the cost price of the asset each year. Depreciation is always given as a percentage. If an asset is depreciated by 15% per annum, then 15% of the cost of the asset is written off as depreciation each year.

Example 12.5

For example, assume that 20% depreciation is written off the value of our table on a straight line basis. This means that the value of the table (cost R300) is depreciated by R60 (or 20%) each year.

Make sure you understand that: R300 × 20% = R60

After one year, the value of the table is reduced (or depreciated) by R60. Since the table cost R300 and we have depreciated it by R60, it is now worth only R240 (R300 − R60). This adjusted value (R240) is called the **book value** of the table. The book value is simply what the table is currently worth according to the accounting records (the books) of the business.

Cost of the table	R300
Less: Depreciation (Yr 1)	R 60
Book value of the table after 1 year	R240

At the end of the second year, the table is depreciated by a further 20% which brings its book value down to R180.

Cost of the table	R300
Less: Depreciation (Yr 1)	R 60
Book value of the table after 1 year	R240
Less : Depreciation (Yr 2)	R 60
Book value of the table after 2 years	R180

Note that by the end of the second year, the accumulated depreciation is R120 (R60 + R60).

At the end of the third year, another R60 is written off the asset and the book value drops to R120. After four years, the book value drops to R60 and by the end of the fifth year, the book value of the table is nil.

The straight line method of depreciation writes off the same amount of depreciation each year. Therefore the book value of the asset drops equally year by year.

Example 12.6

Assume that Bob's Bikes buys a table for R300 on 1 January 1996. The **office furniture** account is debited in the general ledger and the **bank** account (cash book) is credited (assume that Bob paid by cheque).

The office furniture account now appears as follows:

OFFICE FURNITURE				
1996				
Jan 1	Bank	CB1	300,00	

From an accounting point of view, depreciation at 20% per annum on a straight line basis is recorded as follows at the end of the financial year (31 December):

Year 1 (Financial year end 31 December 1996)

JOURNAL OF BOB'S BIKES

Date	Details	Folio	Debit	Credit
1996 Dec 31	Depreciation Accumulated depreciation on office furniture (Depreciation written off office furniture at 20% p.a.)	L19 L22	60,00	60,00

DEPRECIATION — 19

1996 Dec 31 Acc depn J1	60	

ACCUMULATED DEPRECIATION ON OFFICE FURNITURE — 22

	1996 Dec 31 Depreciation J1 60,00

Please note that depreciation is an expense account and therefore it must be debited.

The office furniture account shows us what the asset cost (R300) while the accumulated depreciation account tells us how much has been depreciated off office furniture so far (R60). Therefore, the difference between these two accounts is the book value of the asset at the end of that year.

> Office furniture (cost) – Accumulated depreciation on office furniture = Book value of the office furniture.

In our example, book value after 1 year = R300 – R60 = R240

F.   JOURNALISING TRANSACTIONS IN AN EXAMINATION

In an examination, you may be expected to journalise a list of transactions. This list may contain some entries that should be recorded in other subsidiary journals such as cash book, sales or purchases journals.

However, you may be asked to enter all the transactions into the general journal, even though they would normally be entered into other subsidiary books.

For example, journalise the following transaction in the books of Bob's Bikes: On 7 March 1996, Bob paid R1 000 for goods.

Date	Details	Folio	Debit	Credit
1996 Mar 7	Purchases Bank (Goods bought for cash)		1 000	1 000

This transaction is normally entered in the Cash Payments section of the cash book of Bob's Bikes. However, an examiner may ask you to enter it into the journal to see if you understand the double entry system.

Test-yourself questions

Exercise 12.1
Journalise the following transactions in the books of Adam & Co:

January

1 Allowed R5 discount to Owen & Co.
2 An amount of R27 was charged to the railage account instead of the repairs account during December and it must be corrected.
3 Sold goods to C. Summer on credit for R155.
4 Purchased goods for resale worth R206 for D. Liver on 30 days terms.
5 Agreed to allow C. Summer 5% discount on the goods he purchased on 3 January.
6 Received notification from Collect and Zappern that they had recovered R100 from Finally & Co which had previously been written off as bad.
7 D. Carator submitted an invoice for R2 500 in respect of painting the exterior of the office building.
8 On the advice of the auditors, it was agreed to create a provision of 5% against bad debts based on total outstanding debtors of R26 840.
9 A refund of R200 received from O. Vernon in respect of an overpayment made in December had been correctly recorded in the cash book but incorrectly posted to the Debtors' control account.
10 Sold goods worth R300 to C. Dover & Co on credit.

Exercise 12.2
You have been employed by Swakop Fisheries to do their books. You are presented with the following information and are asked to:

1. Journalise the transactions
2. Post to the ledger
3. Prepare a trial balance as at 29 February 1992

Use the following ledger accounts:
Accounts payable (creditors); Accounts receivable (debtors); Bank; Capital; Returns inwards (sales returns); Purchases; Stock; Sales; Rent; Wages.

1997
February
1 L. Hake commenced Swakop Fisheries trading with an investment of R800 in stock and R4 200 in cash.
2 Bought goods on credit from Whiting and Sons for R1 200.
3 Cash sales, R250.
  Sales on credit to Kabeljou Incorporated of R55.
4 Paid rent of R300.
5 Paid wages of R250.
6 Bought goods for cash, R450.
10 Cash sales, R125.
  The following clients purchased on account:
    Snoek Industrials R220
    Yellowtail CC   R145
12 Paid Whiting and Sons, R800
15 Bought goods on credit from Shark CC for R850.
16 Received R50 from Kabeljou Incorporated in full settlement of their account.
17 Cash sales, R2 250.
20 Yellowtail CC returned goods worth R45.
23 Settled Shark CC's account and claimed 10% discount.

Exercise 12.3

Journalise the following transactions in the books of Adam and Sons. Post to the appropriate ledger accounts.

February
1 Sold goods on credit to Noah Stores, R550.
2 Agreed to allow Ham & Son a discount on their account which was paid on Jan 31, R10,50.
3 Purchased goods on credit from Cain and Co, R600.
4 Items valued at R150 which were previously purchased from Cain and Co were returned as they were found to be defective.
5 Bought a new delivery truck on credit from Ark Transport, R20 000.
6 Received notification from the lawyers that Able had died and that the business would not be able to collect the outstanding amount of R500 from the estate of the deceased debtor.
7 Received a letter from Ark Transport advising that they had agreed to allow Adam and Sons a special discount of 5% on the truck which had just been bought.
8 Sold an old typewriter on credit to Shep Student for R100.
9 Adam took stock valued at R60 home for his personal use.
10 A customer, Jay Pet Supplies, advised that an invoice for R200 charged to his account was actually for goods Adam and Sons had sold to Kay Pet Stores.
11 Rent paid in January of R1 000 had been posted in error to the rent received account. Correct this error.
12 Goods worth R500 were sold to the Red Cross society at a price of R250. Adam and Sons treated the difference as a charitable donation.

Exercise 12.4
Record the following transactions in the journal of Windsor Green Grocer. Post to the appropriate ledger accounts.

1   Bought 300 bags of fruit and vegetables for R3 150 and paid by cheque no. 24 dated 4 March 1991.
2   Placed the following advertisements in *The Star* for the week ended 8 March 1991:
     Shop assistant needed R35
     Grape special advertisement R65
3   Sold R550 on credit to J. Da Silva on 16 March.
4   On 16 March, received the account from Fairland Meat Market for February 1991 made up of:
          Meat delivered to A. Perriera (owner of Windsor Green Grocer) at home, R132.
          Meat for employee lunches, R178.
5   Banked cash sales for the month to date R15 350 on 20 March.
6   Bought 20 bags of carrots from Cresta Vegies on credit for R460 on 21 March.
7   Received R200 from J. Da Silva.
8   Bought a new weighing machine for R1 250 and paid a 10% deposit on 25 March with cheque no. 25. The balance is to be paid over six months to RSA Weights CC.

The expense accounts in the books of Windsor Green Grocers are: Advertising; labour costs; salaries; general expenses; postage and delivery expenses.

Exercise 12.5
Journalise the following transactions (including cash transactions) in the books of F. Mercury, a dealer in washing machines and accessories. Post to the appropriate ledger accounts.

April
3   Bought household groceries for Mrs Mercury from D. John on credit for R40,36.
5   Bought 12 washing machines from B. George for R340 each, less 10% trade discount and paid for eight of them, arranging that the balance would be paid in 1 month's time.
6   Received a cheque for C. Richard for R76 in payment of his account, less 5% discount.
8   Sold 2 washing machines for R800 cash.
10   Mr Mercury took a washing machine which he could have sold for R400 and gave it to an orphanage as a donation. The washing machine originally cost him R275.
11   Mr Jackson returned a machine which he had originally bought on credit for R400.
12   Received notification from the credit manager that he had received a letter from a firm of attorneys advising the business that J. Warble had died and that it was not expected that his estate would be able to settle his account of R516 owing to Mr Mercury.

Exercise 12.6

Journalise the following transactions in the books of B. Bandana. (Narrations are not required.)

February 1997

1   Sold goods on credit to A. Adam for R110.
2   Wrote off a bad debt of a debtor, E. Eve, R202.
3   Rent of R350 paid in January had been incorrectly posted to the Railage account and needs to be corrected.
4   Issued a credit note to A. Adam for 10% discount on the goods sold to him on 1 February.
5   Agreed to pay C. Cane interest of R45 on money owing to him.
6   Bought goods worth R700 on credit from A. Able and received a 10% trade discount.
7   January's Returns Inwards totalling R777 had been incorrectly posted to Returns Outwards. This must be corrected.
8   Wrote off depreciation for 6 months at 20% on a motor vehicle which had been bought for R45 000.
9   Purchased an office typewriter from M. Machine and agreed to pay for this at R300 per month for the next four months.
10 Provide for February's railage account which is expected to be R180.
11 A robbery occurred on the previous night and the new typewriter bought on 9 February was stolen. B. Bandana did not have insurance.
12 Returned R120 worth of goods purchased on 6 February as they were defective and received a credit note.

CHAPTER THIRTEEN

Final Statements

A.   INTRODUCTION

Once the trial balance has been drawn up and all adjusting journal entries have been put through, we can take out the final statements of the business. There are two major financial statements — the income statement and the balance sheet. This lecture deals briefly with these two important statements.

B.   THE INCOME STATEMENT

In Chapter 2, we introduced the concept of profit. Profit is simply the difference between income and expenses. If income exceeds expenses then the business makes a profit. However, if expenses exceed income, then the business makes a loss. If income and expenses are equal, then the business "breaks-even".

The income statement is made up of incomes and expenses

The income statement is drawn up to determine how much profit or loss the business makes. A business must make a profit in order to give the owner(s) some return on their capital investment. Moreover, if a business is not profitable, it will not survive in the long run.

The income statement determines the profit performance of the business and this is very important for both management and shareholders of the business. The income statement is always drawn up for a particular period of time (one month, one quarter, six months or one year). This is because profit must be linked to a period of time. It means nothing that a business made R1 000 profit. Rather we must state the period over which the profit was made. For example, the business made R1 000 profit for the month of January 1997.

The income statement for a trading business is set out as follows:

INCOME STATEMENT OF LUKANI STORES FOR MONTH ENDED JANUARY 1997

Sales		1 000
Less: Cost of sales		600
Opening stock	300	
Purchases	400	
Carriage inwards	100	
	800	
Less: Closing stock	200	
GROSS PROFIT		400
Add: Operating income		320
Rent received	150	
Discount received	170	
		720
Less: Operating expenses		580
Advertising	50	
Depreciation	30	
Electricity and water	120	
Rent	200	
Salaries	180	
NET PROFIT		140

The income statement can be divided into two sections:

1. The Trading section of the income statement

This section of the income statement determines how much gross profit was made. This is the difference between **sales** and the **cost of the goods sold** (cost of sales). In the example, goods to the value of R1 000 were sold. Since these goods cost the business R600, a gross profit of R400 was made. Gross profit is simply the profit that the business makes from buying goods at one price and selling them at a higher price.

Take note that the cost of sales is made up of opening stock plus purchases plus carriage inwards less closing stock.

2. The Profit and Loss section of the income statement

This section of the income statement comprises all other income and all other expenses. Income (other than sales) is added onto the gross profit and expenses (other than purchases and other costs that increase the price of the goods) are subtracted from the gross profit. This leaves the business with a net profit of R140 (R400 + R320 – R580). The net profit is the profit figure by which the performance of the business is assessed.

C. THE BALANCE SHEET

The balance sheet shows what the business owes (liabilities) and what it owns (assets). Therefore, the balance sheet states the financial position of the business at a point in time. The balance sheet gives the assets and liabilities of the business on a particular day — at the end of a financial period.

The balance sheet is made up of assets and liabilities.

The balance sheet is set out as follows:

BALANCE SHEET OF LUKANI STORES ON 31 JANUARY 1997

Capital Employed		
Owner's equity		4 900
Capital balance: 1 January 1997	4 800	
Add: Net profit	140	
Less: Drawings	40	
Long-term liabilities		1 100
Loan from bank	1 100	
		6 000

Employment of capital

Fixed Assets	Cost	Accumulated depreciation	Book value
Furniture	4 000	100	3 900
Investments			1 000
Net Current Assets			1 100
Current assets		1400	
Stock	200		
Debtors	600		
Bank	500		
Expenses prepaid	100		
Less: Current liabilities		300	
Expenses accrued	200		
Creditors	100		
			6 000

Owner's equity is the amount that the business "owes" to its owner(s). Remember that you should think of this as the liability that the business has to its owner(s). The owner's equity is the result of adding capital (R4 800) and net profit (R140) and subtracting drawings (R40).

D. FUNDAMENTAL ACCOUNTING CONCEPTS

Financial statements are prepared on the basis of four concepts:

The going concern concept
The business is a going concern that will continue to be in existence for the foreseeable future. The income statement and balance sheet must be drawn up to assume that the business will continue to operate.

Matching concept
Income and expenses are recorded into the books of the business as they are earned or incurred. We do not distinguish whether it is this year's or next year's income or expense. Nevertheless, income and expenses must be matched to the financial period under consideration. The annual income statement must contain income and expenses that are for that year only. Therefore, if income or expenses are accrued or paid in advance, we must make the necessary adjustments.

Consistency concept
The consistency concept demands that there is a consistency of accounting treatment for similar items within each accounting period and from one period to the next.

Prudence concept
This means that profits should only be recorded when they are realised. If a loss is made, it must be acknowledged immediately or a best estimate of that loss should be recorded. The prudence concept demands that accountants always take the conservative view.

Exercise 13.1

For each of the following indicate with a cross in the table where in the financial statements you would expect to find the balance:

	INCOME STATEMENT		BALANCE SHEET	
	TRADING SECTION	PROFIT/LOSS SECTION	CAPITAL EMPLOYED*	EMPLOY-MENT OF CAPITAL**
Advertising				
Bank overdraft				
Bank charges				
Bank interest paid				
Buildings				
Capital				
Cash				
Creditors				
Carriage inwards				
Carriage outwards				
Commission paid				
Furniture & fittings				
General expenses				
Insurance paid				
Building Society loan				
Motor vehicles				
Vehicle repairs				
Payments in advance				
Purchases				
Rent received				
Salaries				
Stock (end of period)				
Sales				
Wages				

* Capital, or long-term liabilities.

** Assets and current liabilities.

Exercise 13.2

For each of the questions below you are required to state whether the statement is true or false:

1. If a trial balance balances, then no fraud has taken place.
2. The matching concept justifies the usage of accruals and deferrals.
3. Stock is normally a company's most valuable fixed asset.
4. Trade creditors are a source of finance for a company.
5. Turnover is a company's profit before taxation.

6. Cash is the most liquid asset.
7. Long-term liabilities are borrowings on which interest is charged.
8. General ledger is not a book of prime entry.
9. Debtors are suppliers we are indebted to.
10. Income paid in advance is a type of current asset.

Exercise 13.3
Write a sentence to explain the following:
1. Matching concept
2. Going concern concept
3. Prudence concept

Exercise 13.4
For each of the following transactions, indicate which book of prime entry (subsidiary book) it would be entered into:
1. Sales of goods for cash.
2. Purchases of stock on credit.
3. Purchase of capital equipment paid for by cheque.
4. Collection from debtors.
5. Initial capital invested in the business.
6. Depreciation expenses.
7. Payments to creditors.
8. Purchase of a small amount of stationery.
9. Purchase of stock for cash.
10. Sales of goods on credit.

Exercise 13.5
You are presented with the following trial balance of Mdela International at 30 September 1996:

Capital		10 000
Sales		90 000
Creditors		25 000
Debtors	15 000	
Stock (1.10.1995)	50 000	
Purchases	50 000	
Expenses	10 000	
	125 000	125 000

Closing stock R60 000

You are required to calculate the company's gross profit for the year ended 30 September 1996.

CHAPTER FOURTEEN

Reconciliation of Bank Accounts

A. INTRODUCTION

Most businesses run a current account at a bank. Incoming money is deposited into the bank account and the business can make payment by cheque.

The bank also keeps a record of the transactions of the business. At the end of the month, the bank sends a statement showing a list of transactions. This is called a **bank statement**.

This means that two parties keep a record of the money affairs of the business:

1. The business itself will keep a record of "money coming in" in the Receipts section of the cash book, and "money paid out" in the Payments section of the cash book.
2. The bank keeps a record of money deposited into the bank account and cheque payments from the bank account.

For many reasons, the bank balance per the business records (cash book) may be out of step with the bank balance according to the bank's records (bank statement).

In such an instance, we must be able to explain any differences between the two sets of records. This explanation is called a **bank reconciliation statement**.

B. THE BANK STATEMENT

As part of their service, banks supply their clients with a bank statement on a regular basis. This is a list of transactions over a specified period, usually one month. The opening bank balance increases with any deposit of money into the bank and decreases by withdrawals or payments of money. Usually a running balance is given, reflecting the new balance after each transaction. The final balance is the closing balance on the client's account according to the records of the bank.

The wrong way around?
The bank debits the client's account for all cash payments. The bank credits the client's account for all cash receipts. You may well jump up and down and say that this is wrong — the bank does not understand the double entry system. But it is correct!

Remember that when you write up the books of a business, you will debit the bank when money is deposited. This is because the asset (bank) is increasing. But from the bank's point of view, their liabilities are increasing since they now owe you, the client, more money. Therefore, in the bank's records, your deposits are credits (liabilities).

When you write up the books of a business, you will credit the bank when money is paid out. This is because the asset (bank) is decreasing. But from the bank's point of view, their liabilities are decreasing since they now owe you, the client, less money. Therefore, in the bank's records, your payments are debits (reducing their liability to you).

C. A DIFFERENCE BETWEEN CASH BOOK AND BANK RECORDS

When a business receives the bank statement from the bank, it must compare the balance per bank statement with the balance reflected in its own records. If there is a difference between the two balances, the business must be able to explain why the difference exists. In other words, the difference between the balances must be reconciled.

There are a number of likely REASONS why the records of the business and the bank may differ:

1. Transactions not yet entered in the cash book

A number of items may appear on the bank statement that are not yet entered into the cash book or are incorrectly shown in the cash book.

(a) *Bank charges*

Any charges in respect of service fees or interest on overdraft are automatically deducted from the client's account. This means that these charges first come to the attention of the client on receiving a copy of the bank statement.

Please note that all charges levied by the bank are collectively called bank charges, except for interest on overdraft which is recorded separately.

(b) *Stop orders*

A stop order is an instruction to the bank to make a regular payment on behalf of the client to a specified payee. For example, a monthly payment for insurance could be arranged through a stop order. This saves having to write out a cheque each month and send it to the insurer. The bank automatically transfers the money from the client's account to the payee each month.

Confirmation that the stop order has been executed is obtained through the bank statement.

(c) *Direct deposits*

Money may be directly deposited into a business's bank account by a debtor. This transaction may only come to the attention of the business on receipt of their bank statement.

(d) *Errors in the Cash Receipts or Cash Payments section of the cash book*

Any errors in the cash book of the business will disturb the balance between the bank account and bank statement balance. With regard to all these differences the following approach must be taken:

> ONCE THE BANK STATEMENT IS RECEIVED, YOU MUST FIND ALL SUCH ITEMS THAT ARE NOT YET ENTERED INTO THE BUSINESS RECORDS. THESE MUST NOW BE ENTERED INTO THE CASH BOOK.

This brings the cash book up to date with the bank's records.

2. Transactions not yet entered by the bank in the bank statement

Some transactions are entered into the cash book but are not reflected, or are incorrectly shown, in the bank statement.

(a) *Outstanding deposits*
Money deposited at the end of the month of January will appear in the January cash book. However, since the bank takes a day or so to process the deposit, it only appears on the February bank statement. At the end of January, this deposit is called an outstanding deposit.

(b) *Outstanding cheques*
On the date of writing out a cheque, the payment is entered into the Cash Payments section of the cash book. The payee may only deposit the cheque some days later. The cheque payment only comes to the attention of your bank once the payee deposits the cheque. Therefore, some cheques that are issued in January only go through your bank account in February. At the end of January, these are called outstanding cheques.

(c) *Errors on the bank statement*
An error may be made on the bank statement. This also causes a difference between the records of the bank and the business. With regard to all these differences, the following approach must be taken:

ONCE THE BANK STATEMENT IS RECEIVED, YOU MUST FIND ALL SUCH ITEMS THAT ARE NOT YET ON THE STATEMENT. THESE MUST NOW BE SHOWN ON THE BANK RECONCILIATION STATEMENT.

The bank reconciliation statement explains any disagreement between cash book balance and bank statement balance.

D.   RECONCILING THE BUSINESS BANK ACCOUNT TO THE BANK STATEMENT

1.   Compare the cheque payments in the bank statement with the cheque payments on the credit side of the cash book. Tick off those items that are common to both bank statement and cash book.
2.   Compare the deposits in the bank statement with the cash receipts on the debit side of the cash book. Tick off those items that are common to both bank statement and cash book.
3.   Those items that appear in the bank statement but not in the cash book, must be entered into the cash book.
4.   Those items that appear in the cash book but not in the bank statement, must be shown in the bank reconciliation statement.

Example 14.1
The bank reconciliation statement is best explained by means of an example. The information below applies to Eastward High School.

BANK RECONCILIATION STATEMENT AT 31 JANUARY 1996

Balance per bank statement		33 400
Outstanding cheque no 251	500	
Outstanding deposit		1 100
Balance per cash book	34 000	
	34 500	34 500

CASH BOOK OF EASTWARD HIGH SCHOOL FOR FEBRUARY 1996

RECEIPTS SECTION

Date	Details	Sundry	School fees	Discount allowed	Text-books	Bank
Feb 1	Balance b/d	34 000				34 000
3	School fees		250			250
4	Textbooks				80	80
7	School fees		750	20		730
12	Textbooks				110	110
	School fees		250			250
17	School fees		750	20		730
25	Field trip	500				500
28	School fees		250			250
		34 500	2 250	40	190	36 900

PAYMENTS SECTION

Date	Cheq no.	Details	Sundry	Wages	Creditors	Disc rec'd	Bank
Feb 1	254	Telephone	200				200
7	255	Wages		400			400
13	256	Juta's			1 700	50	1 650
15	257	Wages		400			400
19	258	Elec & water	630				630
22	259	Joe's Garage			1 150	30	1 120
	260	Wages		400			400
25	261	Sports World			750		750
27	262	Rates	650				650
28	263	Wages		400			400
	264-270	Salaries	15 600				15 600
			17 080	1 600	3 600	80	22 200

BANK STATEMENT — EASTWARD HIGH SCHOOL

February

Balance brought forward	01 02		33 400
Cheque 251	01 02	500-	32 900
Deposit	01 02	1 100cr	34 000
Deposit	03 02	250cr	34 250
Deposit	04 02	80cr	4 330
Cheque 254	05 02	200-	34 130
Deposit	07 02	730cr	34 860
Cheque 255	07 02	400-	34 460
Deposit	12 02	360cr	34 820
Duty on debit entries	13 02	4-	34 816
Cheque 257	15 02	400-	34 416
Cheque 256	16 02	1 650-	32 766
Deposit	17 02	730cr	33 496
Cheque 258	20 02	630-	32 866
Direct deposit — T. Vos	21 02	250cr	33 116
Cheque 260	22 02	400-	32 716
Cheque 259	24 02	1 120-	31 596
Deposit	25 02	500cr	32 096
Service fee	26 02	14-	32 082
Cheque 261	28 02	750-	31 332
Cheque 263	28 08	400-	30 932CR

The direct deposit on 21 February was for payment of the school fees of Harry Vos.

Required:
1. Complete the cash book for February 1996.
2. Draw up a bank reconciliation statement at 28 Feb 1996.

Solution to Example 14.1
You must go through each of the following steps and do what is asked. Then compare your answer to the solution as you go along.

Step 1
Tick off the receipts in the Cash Receipts section of the cash book against the receipts shown on the bank statement. Remember to look in the previous month's reconciliation to see if there are any receipts that you can tick off against the current bank statement. In this example, there is an outstanding deposit of R1 100.

Step 2
Tick off the cheque payments in the cash payments section of the cash book against the payments shown on the bank statement. Remember to look in the previous month's reconciliation to see if there are any cheques that you can tick off against the current bank statement. In this example, there is an outstanding cheque no. 251 for R500.

Step 3

Circle those items in the Cash Receipts section that are not ticked. You should have circled the last amount of R250 for school fees on 28 February. (The balance b/d should be ignored.)

Step 4

Circle those items in the Cash Payments section that are not ticked. You should have circled R650 (cheque 262) and R15 600 (cheques 264 – 270).

Step 5

Circle those items in the bank statement that are not ticked. You should have circled R4 (13 02), R250cr (21 02) and R14 (26 02).

Step 6

You are now ready to complete the cash book. Those entries in the bank statement that are circled must be recorded into the cash book.

The present balance in the cash book can be worked out by subtracting the total of the Payments section from the total of the Receipts section (R36 900 – R22 200 = R14 700). Since the school has received more money than it has spent, this is a favourable (debit) balance.

In order to complete the cash book for February, the three circled entries in the bank statement must be included in this cash book balance.

DR	COMPLETE CASH BOOK OF EASTWARD SCHOOL (SUPPLEMENTARY CASH BOOK)					CR
Feb			Feb			
28	Balance b/d	14 700,00	28	Bank charges		18,00
	School fees	250,00		(R4 + R14)		
	(Harry Vos)			Balance c/d		14 932,00
		14 950,00				14 950,00
	Balance b/d	14 932,00				

Step 7

In the last step, we draw up the bank reconciliation statement for February 1996. This is done to account for the difference between the updated cash book balance (R14 932) and the bank statement balance (R30 932). Four items are required in this regard:

1. The cash book balance (from step 6)
2. The bank statement balance (the last figure in the balance column)
3. The outstanding deposits (the circled amounts in the cash receipts section)
4. The outstanding cheques (the circled amounts in the cash payments section)

	Debit	Credit
Balance per bank statement		30 932
Outstanding cheques		
No 262	650	
No 264 – 270	15 600	
Outstanding deposit		250
Balance per cash book	14 932	
	31 182	31 182

Notes on the above bank reconciliation statement:

1. Since the cash book has a debit (favourable balance), the balance is shown in the debit column.
2. Outstanding cheques are always shown in the debit column.
3. Outstanding deposits are always shown in the credit column.
4. Since the bank statement has a credit balance, it is shown in the credit column.
5. We know that the bank statement and cash book agree when the totals on the bank reconciliation statement are equal.

Exercise 14.1
The following information is extracted from the records of Butch Industries:

Bank reconciliation as at 28 February 1995

Balance per cash book		R6 902
Plus outstanding cheques		
No 338	810	
No 340	1 203	
No 341	25	
No 342	475	
No 343	30	
No 345	79	2 622
Less deposits not yet credited:		
27 February 1995	1 000	
28 February 1995	753	1 753
Balance per bank statement		7 771

CASH BOOK OF BUTCH INDUSTRIES FOR MARCH 1995

(Bank columns only are given)

Date	Details	Bank	Date	Cheq	Details	
Mar 1	Balance b/d	6 902	Mar 2	387	Wages	120
5	Goofy Systems	4 300	10	388	Rent	895
12	Chippy Tools	581		389	Elec & water	12 530
13	Porky Stores	63		390	Purchases	3 955
17	Ernie Ent	585	13	391	Wages	7 596
19	Jaws and Co	7 233	17	392	Purchases	8 102
20	Goofy Systems	5 129	20	393	Purchases	30 000
	Gore and Son	280	22	394	F Dufour	5 416
22	J. Lewis	289		395	Equipment	5 000
23	Felix & James	4 363	23	396	Drawings	10 000
	V. Ford	5 966		397	J Preston	9 049
27	PH Labs	5 697	27	398	Entertain	516
30	Gore and Son	9 548		399	Petty Cash	200
31	Goofy Systems	6 325				
	Balance c/d	35 998				
		93 379				93 379

Bank statement for March 1995

Details	Transaction	Date	Balance
BALANCE BROUGHT FORWARD		01.03	7 771
Deposit	1 000 CR	01.03	8 771
Deposit	753 CR	01.03	9 524
Cheque 345	79	01.03	9 445
Bank charges	11	01.03	9 434
Cheque 338	810	03.03	8 624
Deposit	4 300 CR	05.03	12 924
Cheque 387	120	05.03	12 804
Cheque 388	895	10.03	11 909
Cheque 389	12 530	11.03	OD 621
Deposit	581 CR	12.03	OD 40
Service Fee	13	12.03	OD 53
Deposit	63 CR	13.03	10
Deposit	585 CR	17.03	595
Cheque 392	8 046	17.03	OD 7 451
Deposit	7 233 CR	19.03	OD 218
Cheque 391	7 596	19.03	OD 7 814
Service fee	11	19.03	OD 7 825
Deposit	5 129 CR	20.03	OD 2 696
Deposit	280 CR	20.03	OD 2 416
Cheque 393	30 000	21.03	OD 32 416

Cheque 341	25	22.03	OD 32 441
Cheque 394	5 416	22.03	OD 37 857
Deposit	289 CR	22.03	OD 37 568
Deposit	4 363 CR	23.03	OD 33 205
Deposit	5 966 CR	23.03	OD 27 239
Cheque 397	9 049	23.03	OD 36 288
Deposit	5 697 CR	27.03	OD 30 591
Service Fee	7	28.03	OD 30 598
Cheque 396	10 000	29.03	OD 40 598
Cheque 399	200	30.03	OD 40 798
Interest	43	31.03	OD 40 841

You are required to do a bank reconciliation statement for Butch Industries as at 31 March 1995.

Exercise 14.2

During February 1996, the following entries were recorded in the cash book of New Venture:

Date	Details	Bank	Date	Cheq	Details	Bank
Feb 1	Balance b/d	698,40	Feb 1	301	Rent	200,00
7	Debtors	1 066,25	3	302	Drawings	302,50
14	Cash sales	209,50	10	303	Petty cash	50,00
18	Transfer	250,00	11	304	Purchases	392,10
21	Debtors	1 237,60	20	305	Creditors	1885,00
25	Debtors	683,25	23	307	Postage	28,90
27	Cash sales	174,40	25	308	Salaries	764,20
28	Interest	4,65	28		Stop order	18,00
			28	309	Telephone	53,40

Early in March, the Second Provincial Bank sent New Venture a statement which reflected the following transactions:

Details	Transaction	Date	Balance
BALANCE BROUGHT FORWARD		01.02	851,80
Cheque 280	53,40	01.02	798,40
Cheque 301	200,00	01.02	598,40
Cheque 302	302,50	01.02	95,90
Deposit	1 066,25 CR	07.02	1 362,15
Cheque 296	100,00	07.02	1 262,15
Cheque 303	50,00	14.02	1 212,15
Transfer	250,00 CR	18.02	1 462,15
Deposit	1 237,60 CR	21.02	2 699,75
Deposit	683,25 CR	25.02	3 383,00
Cheque 305	1 885,00	25.02	1 498,00
Cheque 308	764,20	25.02	33,80

Cheque 306	250,00	25.02	483,80
Stop order	18,00	28.02	465,80
Interest	4,65 CR	28.02	470,45

You are required to prepare a bank reconciliation statement as at the end of February 1996.

Exercise 14.3

Phindalozi Corporation Ltd needs a bank reconciliation for August 1996, its year end, and their bookkeeper is able to provide you with the following information from her cash book and from the bank statements:

Cheques paid by the bank in August 1996	R8 121,60
Cheques not yet presented for payment	639,20
Cheques drawn in August 1996	8 760,80
Deposits credited by the bank in August 1996	R7 520,00
Deposits credited by the bank in September 1996	564,00
Deposits made in August 1996	8 084,00
August 1996 bank charges per statement	R 169,20

From the July 1996 cash book, you ascertain:

Cheques paid by the bank in July 1996	R5 489,60
Cheques paid by the bank in August 1996	300,00
Cheques not yet presented for payment	225,60
	6 016,0
Deposits credited by bank in July 1996	R7 369,60
Deposits credited by bank in August 1996	451,20
Deposits made in July 1996	7 820,80
July bank charges, per statement	143,75